ビジネスで使える 英語の1分間スピーチ

小坂貴志
ジョン・ワンダリー

CD BOOK

研究社

はじめに
PREFACE

「プレゼンテーション(略して、プレゼン)」という言葉がよく聞かれるようになりました。人前で話をするスピーチという狭義の意味から、見映えといった全体的なあり方をも含んだ概念のプレゼンは、ビジネスの世界で盛んに使われています。その流行の背景にあるのはビジネスのグローバル化であり、人前でしかも英語である程度まとまった考えを相手にアピールできるかが、必要不可欠なスキルとして現代社会では求められているのです。

ところがその反面、プレゼン大流行は、思わぬところで深刻な事態を招いています。そのひとつとしてとりあげられるのは、Microsoft PowerPoint に代表されるプレゼンツールの過剰使用です。だれもかれもが PowerPoint でのプレゼンの時代。これがなければプレゼンできない、という暗黙の了解があると言っても過言ではないでしょう。

しかし残念なことに、PowerPoint 活用はプレゼンのすべてではありません。また、効果的に PowerPoint を使いこなしているケースはまれです。私自身の反省でもありますが、多くの方は聞き手の参照資料となるべき PowerPoint の作り方があまりうまいとはいえません。例外的に美しい PowerPoint の発表にめぐり合うこともあります。でも、そんなときに限って話し手のスピーチがこの上なく聞きづらかったりします。洗練された PowerPoint 資料の内容と話の中味があまりにもかけ離れている事例もあります。いわゆるプレゼンの世界は今や玉石混淆なのです。

なぜこうなってしまったのか。それは、皆さんの頭の中に、プレゼンとは「PowerPoint の資料だけ作って、少し練習すればいいもの」という考えがあるからです。実際、PowerPoint 資料の作成に膨大な時間をさくものの、できあがってしまえば安心して、その資料を使って練習することはまれではないでしょうか。たとえ練習したとしても、与えられた制限時間内で PowerPoint の資料をいかに多く消化するかということばかりに気をとられているようです。

これではプレゼンの本来の目的を見失っているのではないでしょうか。PowerPoint の資料を披露するだけのプレゼンだとしたら、プレゼンする意味がありません。私はこの傾向に対して深い危惧の念を抱いています。

では本来あるべきプレゼンの姿とは何なのか。ビジネス世界では特に、どのような場面においても、まずは、話し手ありき、がいえるのです。何はなくとも、自分を売り込まなければいけません。自分が何を言いたいのかをしっかり心に刻み込み、そして話す。自分の体で、そして自分の目で相手に話し、訴えかける。それを達成するには、PowerPointの資料はあくまでプレゼンの「補助」でしかありえません。なぜなら、話し手より目立ってはいけないからです。

　そこで登場するのが本書で紹介する「スピーチ」です。自分を売り込むためのツールとして最適なのは、話し手の存在感を失くしてしまうPowerPointではなく、話し手の中からにじみ出てくるスピーチなのです。スピーチは自分のすべてをさらけ出して相手と向かい合います。スピーチの最中、聴衆の目は話し手だけに注がれます。スピーチがうまくいけば、話す内容も、話し手の様子もすべて聞き手にインプットされるのです。

　これがPowerPointだったらどうでしょうか。聴衆はPowerPointの資料は覚えていても、話し手個人については無関心ということも考えられるでしょう。ですから、PowerPoint大流行の今にこそ求められるのは、プレゼンという流行に流されず、自分を売り込むためのスピーチに専念すること。PowerPointの効果的な使用法を学ぶのは、その後からでも決して遅くはありません。プレゼンの基本はスピーチにこそあるのです。

　それには、スピーチの目的、構成、内容、場面、表現を吟味することから始めましょう。本書は、スピーチの基礎についての解説書であり、もうすこし欲張って、「そんなことしている余裕がないので、この場合これだ！」という即席サンプル集としてもお使いいただけます。

　「基礎編」では、スピーチの目的、構成について重点的に考えていきます。「実例編」では、目的、構成の理解を踏まえ、さまざまな状況に応じたスピーチのサンプルと豊富な表現を取り揃えています。PowerPointは後回しとはいうものの、プレゼンツールの使い方を知っている人材が求められる時代では、ツールを完全に無視するわけにはいきません。「基礎編」と「実例編」の掛け渡しとして、プレゼンツールを簡単に紹介し、スピーチの補助役として効果的な英語プレゼンツール資料作りの方法を説明しています。

　「索引」のないサンプル集を英語の初心者に渡すのは、泳ぎの初心者に対して荒海の中に飛び込めと言っているようなもの。一般のサンプル集には「索引」が用意されていないものがかなりあります。本書では、皆さんがビジネスの世界でおぼれないよう「索引」をつけましたので、辞書と思って機会を見つけてご利用ください。

はじめに

　さて、本書ができあがるまでの間、多くの方のお世話になりました。すべての方のお名前をあげるわけにはいきませんので、この場を借りて、研究社編集部の吉田尚志さんにお礼の言葉を一言。毎回私の気まぐれな提案に真剣に耳を傾け、それが少しでも現実のものになるよう軌道修正していただいています。そんな作業が本書で5回目となりました。今回も私の力不足で脱稿が延び延びとなったにも関わらず、じっと待ち続けてくださり、このような形で完成品を読者の皆さんにお届けできるのも、ひとえに吉田さんの忍耐力あるのみ、と心より感謝申し上げます。

　読者の皆さんには、ぜひ本書を手にとって、お仕事にフル活用していただきたいと願っています。それでは、皆さんの今後のご活躍をお祈りしております。

　　　　　　　　　　　　　　　　　　　　　　猛暑の大泉学園にて
　　　　　　　　　　　　　　　　　　　　　　著者を代表して
　　　　　　　　　　　　　　　　　　　　　　小坂貴志

目 次
CONTENTS

基礎編　　　　　　　　　　　　　　　　　　　　　　　　　Basics

1. スピーチの目的　　　　　　　　　　　　　　　　　　　　2
　　i　相手にわかりやすく伝える　　　　　　　　　　　　　　3
　　ii　相手を知る　　　　　　　　　　　　　　　　　　　　　4
　　iii　相手を説得する　　　　　　　　　　　　　　　　　　　5
　　iv　相手を楽しませる　　　　　　　　　　　　　　　　　　6

2. スピーチの構成　　　　　　　　　　　　　　　　　　　　7
　　i　Introduction　　　　　　　　　　　　　　　　　　　　8
　　ii　Body　　　　　　　　　　　　　　　　　　　　　　　　9
　　iii　Conclusion　　　　　　　　　　　　　　　　　　　　10

3. スピーチライティング　　　　　　　　　　　　　　　　11
　　i　アウトラインの作成　　　　　　　　　　　　　　　　　12
　　ii　アウトラインのサンプル　　　　　　　　　　　　　　　13
　　iii　スピーチのためのチェックリスト　　　　　　　　　　14

4. PowerPoint 文書の作成　　　　　　　　　　　　　　　15
　　i　PowerPoint 文書を英語でつくる!　　　　　　　　　　16
　　ii　英語プレゼン文書のサンプル　　　　　　　　　　　　17
　　iii　プレゼンの準備　　　　　　　　　　　　　　　　　　28
　　iv　プレゼン準備のためのチェックリスト　　　　　　　　29

実例編　Samples

TOPIC 1	新入社員の自己紹介	32
TOPIC 2	後任者の紹介 ——インフォーマル（くだけたスタイルで）	36
TOPIC 3	後任者の紹介 ——フォーマル（あらたまったスタイルで）	39
TOPIC 4	新入社員を歓迎する	42
TOPIC 5	日本へようこそ！——歓迎のスピーチ	45
TOPIC 6	工場見学 ——始めの挨拶	49
TOPIC 7	送別会のスピーチ ——転任者の送別	52
TOPIC 8	会社の創立記念 ——ひと言挨拶	56
TOPIC 9	忘年会でのスピーチ	59
TOPIC 10	親睦会 ——花見の宴会	63
TOPIC 11	親睦会 ——新年会	66
TOPIC 12	退職 I ——送ることば	69
TOPIC 13	退職 II ——最後の挨拶	73
TOPIC 14	激励するスピーチ I	76
TOPIC 15	激励するスピーチ II	79
TOPIC 16	企業概要 I ——自動車業界	83
TOPIC 17	企業概要 II ——製薬業界	86
TOPIC 18	企業概要 III ——エコツアー会社	89
TOPIC 19	企業概要 IV ——化学物質メーカー	92
TOPIC 20	顧客訪問 ——サービスの説明	95
TOPIC 21	説得 I ——セールストーク	99

TOPIC 22	説得 II ――人事	102
TOPIC 23	新営業所開設 ――発表	106
TOPIC 24	工場閉鎖 ――発表	110
TOPIC 25	支店開設 ――お知らせ	114
TOPIC 26	日本からの代表団が海外の企業へ行く	118
TOPIC 27	日本からの代表団への歓迎スピーチ	122
TOPIC 28	プロジェクト開始 ――ミーティングでの挨拶	126
TOPIC 29	プロジェクト最新状況 ――ミーティングでの挨拶	129
TOPIC 30	プロジェクト完了 ――結果報告	133
TOPIC 31	調査結果の報告	136
TOPIC 32	ボーナスの報告	139
TOPIC 33	解雇の通達	142
TOPIC 34	ブレーンストーミングでの挨拶	145
TOPIC 35	お知らせ ――ミーティングの最後に	149
TOPIC 36	会社の社会奉仕について説明する	152
TOPIC 37	朝礼の挨拶	156
TOPIC 38	株主総会 I ――株価動向	159
TOPIC 39	株主総会 II ――合併のお知らせ	163
TOPIC 40	株主総会 III ――株式分割のお知らせ	166
TOPIC 41	四半期報告	169

索 引 　　　　　　　　　　　　　　　　　　　　　　　　　173

Basics

基礎編

1 スピーチの目的

2 スピーチの構成

3 スピーチライティング

4 PowerPoint 文書の作成

1 スピーチの目的

1 スピーチの目的

i 相手にわかりやすく伝える
ii 相手を知る
iii 相手を説得する
iv 相手を楽しませる

出 典
Dance, F. E. X. & Zak-Dance, C. C. (1986) Public Speaking, Harper & Row, Publishers, New York: NY.

1-i 相手にわかりやすく伝える

▶ 論理展開を把握する
▶ わかりやすい説明とは

▶英語と日本語の論理展開の違いで最も大きなもののひとつに、結論をどこで述べるかということがあげられます。日本語の場合、文章を最後まで聞かないと明確な結論が判別できません。英語のスピーチに、日本語の論理展開をそのまま移植したら、つまり、言いたいことを後回しにしていたのでは、聴衆にそのポイントが伝わりにくくなります。

▶わかりやすい説明をするには、まず言いたいことをいちばん始めに言ってしまう。そして大切な情報を伝達してしまいましょう。スピーチの目的をはっきりと聴衆に伝えることが大切です。相手にわかりやすい論理展開で話すことが必要になります。

1-ii 相手を知る

▶ 自分が言ってみることで情報を得る
▶ 繰り返し言ってみる

▶こちらから情報を提供すると、比較的簡単に情報を聞き出すことができます。ちょっとした隠しごとを思い切って相手に伝える。そうすると、相手から同じような内容の話を聞き出すことができます。聴衆からの意見を聞くには、まず自分が話をする。自分の意見に対して、相手がどう思ってくれるか。全員の前で、自分の調査した事項を聞いてもらって、それに対して感想をもらう。手順がわからないとか、答えが間違っているなど、いろいろなフィードバックが返ってきます。質疑応答では、積極的に情報を収集したいものです。

▶自分が何の情報を得たいのか、そのためには何がポイントになっているのかを繰り返し説明します。イントネーションを変えて言ったり、あるいは、特定の単語を強調したりすることで、より一層の効果が生まれます。スピーチの始めと、終わりの方で繰り返すこともできます。そうすると、スピーチにまとまりがでてきて、話し手が何を欲しているのか、メッセージは何であったのかを長い間、覚えておいてくれるようになります。

1-iii 相手を説得する

▶ 論点をしっかり持つ
▶ そのための事前調査は入念に

▶相手を説得するには、まず論点、内容をしっかり組み立て、それに対して十分な証拠を用意します。説得のためのスピーチは十分な準備と練習が必要となります。いきなり人の心を動かすというのは、難しいでしょう。まずは自分の言っていることに耳を傾けてもらうためのスピーチだとお考えください。はっきりと論理立てて自分の言いたいことを説明する。それがまずは説得する際の第1目標となります。

▶調査をとおしてできるだけ情報を収集しておくことも大切です。できるだけ適切で多くの証拠を用意しておけば説得力が倍増します。

1-iv 相手を楽しませる

▶ 相手を楽しい気分にさせる
▶ 自分も楽しい気分になる

▶楽しませるといってもその幅は広く、ある聴衆は知的に楽しめることを、また別の聴衆は、ただ単に笑わせてくれればいいと思っている場合もあるでしょう。前者は、ノーベル文学賞受賞者によるスピーチ、後者は漫才や落語など、お茶の間的、古典的なスピーチがあたります。

▶相手を楽しませるには、自分が楽しい気分になること。聴衆を見渡して、にっこりと微笑むくらいの余裕をみせると、気持ちがほぐれ、安心してこれからのスピーチに臨めます。

2 スピーチの構成

2 スピーチの構成

i　Introduction
ii　Body
iii　Conclusion

まとまった考えを効果的に聴衆に伝えるには、一定の構成のもとに話を進めます。組み立ては、Introduction, Body, Conclusion の3つです。それぞれの目的、ポイントについて説明していきましょう。

2-i Introduction

イントロダクションとは、スピーチの出だし部分のことで、スピーチ全体の約5分の1(20%)程度の長さを占めています。

イントロダクションの目的として、スピーチに関係するその日の自分の調子を知ることがあげられます。それには、まず自分の声をよく聞いてみることです。また、スピーチの目的を提示することも重要です。キーセンテンスは完全に暗記するくらいの覚悟で、イントロダクションで言ってしまいましょう。印象づけをすることも、その後のスピーチの出来を決める大切な要素です。姿勢を正して、1度深呼吸してから、聴衆全員にアイコンタクトすれば、印象はとてもよくなります。

2-ii Body

ボディとは、スピーチの本体部分のことで、自分の言いたいことを証明するためにあります。通常、スピーチ全体の約5分の3（60％）の長さを占めています。

自分の言いたいことを証明するには、しっかりと証拠を提示することが大切です。あまり多くの点について話しても意味がありませんので、ポイントを3つ程度に絞りましょう。スピーチの目的がいかに聴衆に関係するかを説得することも忘れてはなりません。聴衆の視点に立って、双方向コミュニケーションをお忘れなく。

2-iii Conclusion

コンクルージョンとは、スピーチの最後を締めくくるもので、
目的やポイントについての説明、
印象づけを再度行ないます。
スピーチ全体の約5分の1（20％）を占めます。

聴衆の理解度をより高めるため、ポイントを再度まとめ、疑問点がありそうだったらそれに言及しましょう。聴衆の気持ちを動かすには、何はなくとも「アイコンタクト」です。印象的に終えるには、リハーサルを怠りなく、短く勢いよく終わることも大切となります。

3 スピーチライティング

3	**スピーチライティング** ▶ 一字一句書く ▶ アウトラインを書く 　ⅰ　アウトラインの作成 　ⅱ　アウトラインのサンプル 　ⅲ　スピーチのためのチェックリスト

▶一字一句書くのはとても大切な場面でのみ。重要なスピーチなら原稿を読んでも問題ないでしょう。

▶通常のスピーチでしたら、アウトライン（あらまし）だけですませます。ただ、みなさんはまだ慣れていないでしょうから、本書のサンプルをしっかり参考にして、スピーチしてください。

3-i アウトラインの作成

▶ 目的、構成を考える

Date: / /
Occasion: (　　　)

Specific purpose:
Time:　　minutes

Introduction:
Body:

Conclusion:

Notes:

▶構成を考え始める前に、ぜひやっていただきたいのは、スピーチの目的をはっきりさせることです。次にスピーチする状況・構成を考えます。

3-ii アウトラインのサンプル

▶ 具体例を使う

Date: 9/1/07
Occasion: (Welcome party)

Specific purpose: Introducing myself — high school, birthplace, what I would like to do in the future
Time: 3 minutes

Introduction: My name, school in Japan, birthplace

Body: Things I would like to do
1. swimming
2. studying at University of Colorado

Conclusion: Looking forward to seeing everyone

▶ スピーチでは、自分の考えていることをはっきりと伝えることが主眼となります。難しいことを話そうとは思わず、むしろ難しくても少し内容をかみくだいて説明します。具体例、エピソード、比喩などを多用することです。そうすれば、わかりやすく、印象深いスピーチができあがります。

3-iii スピーチのための チェックリスト

	OK	要練習
〈事前準備〉		
スピーチの目的が説明できる	☐	☐
内容に関する調査をした	☐	☐
賛否両論の意見を理解した	☐	☐
引用の出典が明確になっている	☐	☐
アウトラインが手元にある	☐	☐
内容をレビューしてもらった	☐	☐
〈練　習〉		
実際に練習してみた	☐	☐
鏡に向かって練習してみた	☐	☐
アウトラインがなくても話せるようになった	☐	☐
時間制限以内にスピーチが終わった	☐	☐
誰かにスピーチを聴いてもらった	☐	☐
〈言語コミュニケーション面〉		
Ah…, Oh…, など、vocalized pause がない	☐	☐
難しいキーワードの発音を確かめた	☐	☐
〈非言語コミュニケーション面〉		
アイコンタクトがとれる	☐	☐
ジェスチャーが自然に使える（不自然な手の動きがない）	☐	☐
〈当　日〉		
服装が決まっている	☐	☐
会場の場所・行き方を確認した	☐	☐
部屋の状況等を確認した	☐	☐
備品（パソコン、PowerPoint）を確認した	☐	☐

＊（注）確認できたら、☐をチェックしてください。

4 PowerPoint 文書の作成

> ## 4 PowerPoint 文書の作成
>
> ▶ プレゼンツールに頼りすぎるな
> ▶ Microsoft PowerPoint
>   i PowerPoint 文書を英語でつくる!
>   ii 英語プレゼン文書のサンプル
>   iii プレゼンの準備
>   iv プレゼン準備のためのチェックリスト

▶プレゼンツールは視覚支援ツールとして、さまざまな場面で利用されています。従来のソフトでは考えられなかった効果が提供でき、説得力のあるプレゼンを実現してくれます。ただ、100% ツールに頼るのは危険です。ツールがなくてもスピーチできるようにしておきましょう。

▶今や Microsoft PowerPoint がプレゼンツールのスタンダードになっています。PowerPoint のウイザードの説明にしたがって操作すれば、ワープロ感覚で簡単に資料が作れてしまいます。

4-i PowerPoint文書を英語でつくる!

- ▶ 書くのではなく、リストせよ
- ▶ 1ページに3〜5行
- ▶ 1ページに項目は3つまで
- ▶ 箇条書きの英文スタイルを知れ
- ▶ 背景色は明るい色にせよ

英語でどのようなドキュメントを用意したらいいのか。そのポイントをご紹介しておきましょう。

▶自分の言いたいことをすべて書き込むのでは非効果的です。項目をリストアップするような気持ちでつくりましょう。

▶1ページには3〜5行。

▶項目は3つまでとしておきます。

▶英語でリストとくれば、箇条書きです。箇条書きのスタイルについて知っておくのも便利です。

▶背景色は濃い目にすると、全体が引き締まった感じに仕上がるのですが、一方、配布資料用に印刷すると、メモがとれなくなってしまいます。配布資料として使う場合には、背景色の色は明るいものにしておきましょう。もちろん、配布資料として使わないのなら、背景色はさほど問題になりません。

4-ii 英語プレゼン文書のサンプル

▶ 通訳者の使い方
自分の英語で言いたいことが相手に伝わるか不安な方、特に、大切な商談や交渉ごととともなると、やはり通訳者を雇うケースがでてくるでしょう。通訳者だから何でも訳せると通訳者任せにしていると、後で痛い目に合うこともあります。

ここでは、「通訳者の使い方」と題して、PowerPoint ドキュメントを使っての英語スピーチのサンプルを用意しました。英語 PowerPoint ドキュメントの作り方と合わせて、通訳者の使い方について、またはそれを説明するスピーチについてお考えください。

4-ii ❶ How to Use an Interpreter

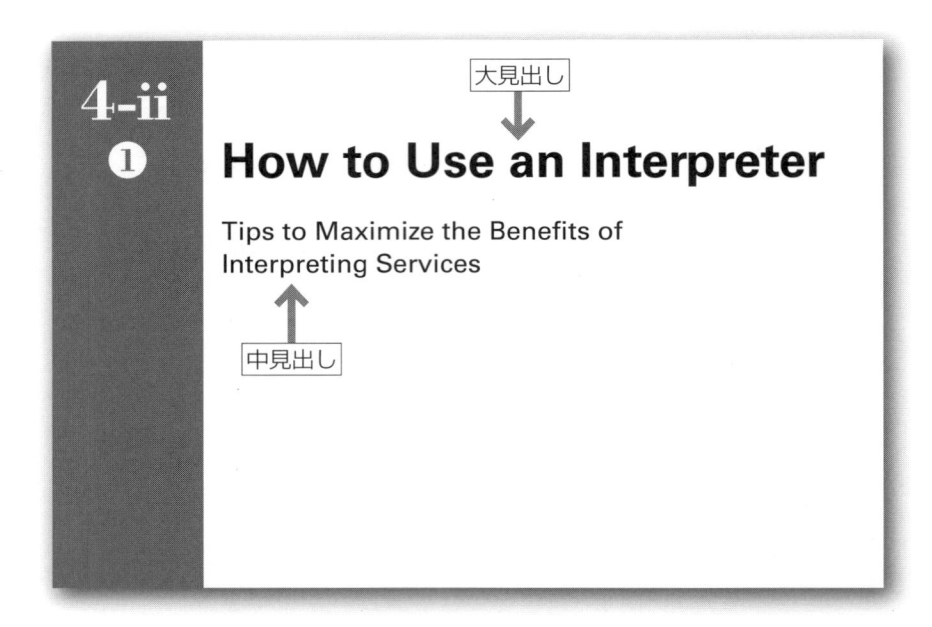

大見出し

Tips to Maximize the Benefits of Interpreting Services

中見出し

> **sample speech:**

Let me show you how to be prepared to work with interpreters in giving presentations. I will teach you some fundamental knowledge about how interpreting works.

▶トップページは、大見出し、中見出しでテーマを紹介します。

4-ii ② Background Information

- What is interpreting?
- Modes of interpreting
- Advantages and disadvantages of each mode

　　　　↑
　　　箇条書き

💬 **sample speech:**
Let's first take a look at what interpreting is and how it works.

▶箇条書きにして、具体的な内容を紹介します。

4-ii ③ What is Interpreting?

Interpreting is the act of listening to information given by the speaker in one language (the source language) and transmitting that information to the listeners in a language that they can understand (the target language).

🗩 **sample speech:**

Interpreting is the act of listening to information given by the speaker in one language (the source language) and transmitting that information to the listeners in a language that they can understand (the target language).

▶定義、引用は PowerPoint に書いてある文章をそのまま読んでも構いません。それ以外の場合は、できるだけ読まないようにしましょう。

4-ii Modes of Interpreting

- Consecutive
- Simultaneous
    Whispering

sample speech:
There are two principal types, or modes of interpreting: Consecutive and simultaneous. Whispering is a subcategory of simultaneous.

4-ii ⑤ Consecutive Interpreting

- Speaker and interpreter speak consecutively tag-team style
- Interpreter takes notes
- Segments last from a few seconds to several minutes

sample speech:

One is consecutive interpreting. This is where the speaker talks for anywhere from a few seconds to up to several minutes while the interpreter listens carefully, sometimes taking notes. The speaker then stops to allow the interpreter to reproduce the message in the target language. Once the interpreter has finished, the speaker then continues with another segment.

4-ii Simultaneous Interpreting
6

- Interpreter and speaker talk at the same time
- Audio equipment such as soundproof booths, headsets and wireless earpieces are used, especially for large groups
- Portable equipment can be used for smaller groups

sample speech:

The other mode of interpreting is simultaneous. Here, audio equipment is used so that the interpreter can relay the message in the target language to the audience while the speaker is presenting the information. The interpreters often work in soundproof booths where they use headphones to hear the speakers and microphones to relay their interpretation to wireless audio receivers worn by those listening to the interpreting. This is suitable for large audiences and limited numbers of speakers, since each speaker must use a microphone that is fed into the interpreting booth.

For smaller meetings, portable equipment can be used for simultaneous interpreting. Here, the interpreter listens to the speaker through the air and transmits the interpretation into a small, hand-held microphone to be heard through wireless audio receivers worn by those listening to the interpretation. This is suitable when the speakers are not using microphones, but where the meeting is taking place in a room small enough that the interpreter can easily hear all of the speakers. This type of interpreting also works well when the information is given while moving, such as on a plant tour.

4-ii Whispering

- Speaker and interpreter talk at the same time
- Usually done with no equipment at all
- Used when target audience is limited to one or two people

sample speech:

There is one other form of simultaneous interpreting that is called whispering. It is used when only one or two people require interpreting. The interpreter sits behind them, simultaneously whispering the interpretation without using audio equipment.

4-ii ⑧ Advantages and Disadvantages

Consecutive 利点　　　　　　　　　不利点

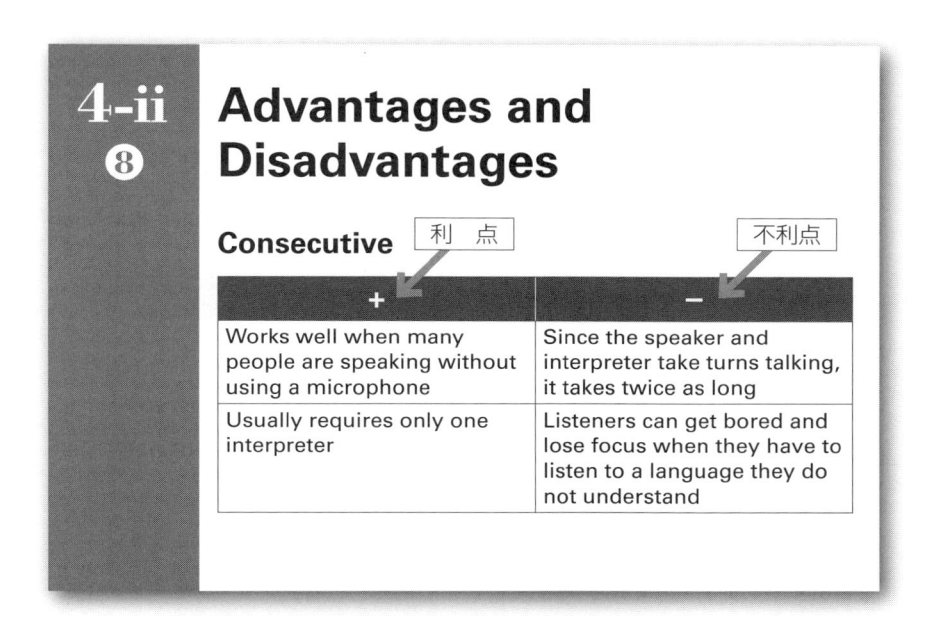

+	−
Works well when many people are speaking without using a microphone	Since the speaker and interpreter take turns talking, it takes twice as long
Usually requires only one interpreter	Listeners can get bored and lose focus when they have to listen to a language they do not understand

💬 **sample speech:**

In deciding what kind of interpreting you will need, use this chart as a reference.

Consecutive interpreting works well in small- to medium-size meetings where various people will be speaking. Comments by anybody in the room can easily be interpreted and no special equipment is required. Meetings of reasonable length can usually be handled by one interpreter. Some of the drawbacks are that a meeting will take about twice as long as it would without interpretation since everything that is said must then be repeated in the target language, doubling the amount of speaking.

For extremely long or intense meetings, such as negotiations, or meetings where perfect accuracy is absolutely essential, it is a good idea to consider hiring at least two interpreters even if using consecutive interpreting.

▶表形式で、利点（＋）、不利点（−）を比較しています。

4-ii ⑨ Advantages and Disadvantages

Simultaneous

+	−
Saves time compared to consecutive since the speaker and interpreter talk at the same time	Usually requires at least two interpreters
Allows interpretation into multiple languages at once	Requires the use of audio equipment

🗩 **sample speech:**

Again, in deciding what kind of interpreting you will need, use this chart as a reference.

The main advantage of simultaneous interpreting is that much time is saved compared to consecutive interpreting since the speaker and the interpreter are speaking at the same time. On the down side, since simultaneous interpreting is usually much more mentally taxing than consecutive, interpreters usually work in pairs, trading off after 15-30 minutes, meaning that two interpreters are usually required.

4-ii ⑩ Advantages and Disadvantages

Whispering

+	−
Can be done without the use of equipment	Can be used only when the target audience is limited to one or two people
Saves time since the speaker and interpreter talk at the same time	Can be disconcerting for those sitting close to the interpreter who are trying to hear the speaker

sample speech:

Whispering is efficient and also easy to arrange logistically since no special equipment is required. However, it is not very practical when there are more than two people who need to hear the interpreting.

4-iii プレゼンの準備

- ▶ 事前準備
- ▶ プレゼンツールの稼動確認

▶実際にプレゼンツールを使う際は事前準備が欠かせません。当日、スピーチの時間が来てから焦り始めなくてもすむように、せめて発表前日までには稼動確認をしておきたいものです。なぜ「当日」ではないか、というと、当日は他の人の発表で会場が使えない場合も考えられるからです。そのためにも、前日の夜がチェックには最適でしょう。プロジェクターが設定されていないのなら、当日の朝早くにでもチェックをすませておけば安心です。

▶稼動確認の項目には、
①ソフトの互換性
②ケーブル・電源類
③プロジェクター
④パソコンとプロジェクターの接続
　があります。

4-iv プレゼン準備のための チェックリスト

	OK	要確認
〈ファイル〉		
日本語が文字化けしないか	□	□
作ったイメージの見映えは大丈夫か	□	□
会場にあるソフトでファイルが読めるか	□	□
〈パソコン単体〉		
パソコン用の電源があるか	□	□
パソコン用のACアダプタを持ったか	□	□
〈プロジェクター単体〉		
プロジェクターがあるか	□	□
プロジェクターまでの電源が確保できるか	□	□
プロジェクターの電球は切れていないか、予備はあるか	□	□
〈パソコンとプロジェクターとの相性〉		
画質は見るに耐えるか	□	□
内部・外部ディスプレイの切り替えができるか	□	□

＊(注)確認できたら、□をチェックしてください。

Samples
実例編

TOPIC 1 新入社員の自己紹介

渡辺恵子さんは大手薬品会社の国際営業部に雇われました。当部署の半数近くの職員が英語を母語とするため、渡辺さんは自己紹介を英語でするように言われました。

Track 1

Good morning. My name is Keiko Watanabe and I have been hired as a market researcher for the North American market. I am delighted to have the opportunity to work with such an excellent group of people.

Let me tell you a bit about myself. My academic background is in business administration with a focus on marketing. I completed my MBA at Columbia University in New York in 2001. I was then recruited by a major advertising firm in New York where I worked as a market research specialist in the pharmaceuticals industry. After nearly six years in the U.S., I decided that I was ready to head back home to Japan and began a job search in Tokyo. It was then that I applied for the position of market researcher here and was thrilled to have been hired. I am very excited about this opportunity to join a company with such a stellar global reputation.

I look forward to getting to know each and every one of you over the coming months while learning as much as possible from the experience that all of you bring to the table. Thank you.

解説

Introduction

自分の名前と職務の説明 → 自己紹介に使える!

Good morning. My name is Keiko Watanabe(名前) and I have been hired as a market researcher(役職) for the North American(ターゲット市場名) market. I am delighted to have the opportunity to work with such an excellent group of people.

> **訳** おはようございます。渡辺恵子と申します。このたび、北米市場の市場調査員として働くことになりました。このような素晴らしい皆様とご一緒に仕事ができますのは、とても光栄です。

> **Notes**
> - 挨拶 → 名前 → 役職 → 感謝
>   挨拶…時間帯によって使い分ける
>   名前…正式な場面では「名前＋姓」
>   役職…職務担当を簡単に述べる
>   感謝…何事も前向きにとらえる
> - be delighted to …　「～できて光栄です」
> - have the opportunity to …　「～の機会をもてる」

Body

自分の履歴(Personal History)を紹介する

Let me tell you a bit about myself. My academic background is in business administration(専攻) with a focus on marketing(興味のある分野). I completed my MBA at Columbia University(大学名) in New York(大学所在地) in 2001(修了年). I was then recruited by a major advertising(業界名) firm in New York(所在地) where I worked as a market research specialist(役職) in the pharmaceuticals(業界名) industry. After nearly six years(就業年数) in the U.S.(就業場所), I decided that I was ready to head back home to Japan(国名) and began a job search in Tokyo(都市名). It was then that I applied for the position of market researcher(役職) here and was thrilled to have been hired. I am very excited about this opportunity to join a company with such a stellar global reputation.

> **訳** 私自身について少しお話ししたいと思います。大学では経営学を、特にマーケティングを学び、2001年にニューヨークのコロンビア大学でMBAを修めました。その後、ニューヨークにあります大手広告会社で薬品市場の市場調査員として働きました。6年近くの米国生活を終え、このたび日本に帰り、東京で就職活動を始めました。そして、この市場調査士の仕事に応

TOPIC 1 新入社員の自己紹介

募し、念願かなって採用されました。世界規模でその名の知られている企業の一員となる機会を与えられましたことをとてもうれしく思います。

Notes
- with a focus on … 「〜に焦点を当てた」
- be recruited by … 「〜に採用される」
- head back home 「帰国する」
- begin a job search 「就職活動を始める」
- join a company 「就職する」
- stellar 「花形の」「一流の」
- 学歴 → 職歴 → 転職の理由
  学歴…大学、大学院を中心に。表現については第2〜3文を参考に
  職歴…企業名は言っても言わなくても可。職務、業界名、年数など
  転職の理由…前向きな理由を言う

Conclusion
よろしくお願いします → 汎用なのでどんな場合にも使える！

I look forward to getting to know each and every one of you over the coming months while learning as much as possible from the experience that all of you bring to the table. Thank you.

訳 これからの数か月のあいだに、ここにいらっしゃるお一人おひとりと知り合い、皆さんの持っておられるご経験から多くの事を学ばせていただけることを楽しみにしています。どうもありがとうございました。

Notes
- bring to the table 「持ち込む」

TOPIC 1 新入社員の自己紹介

POINT ❶
「ご迷惑おかけします」を英語では?

「これから大変ご迷惑をおかけいたしますが…」や「この仕事に対してまだ何も知識がありませんが…」をそのまま訳すと、"I know I am going to cause you so much troubles, but…" とか "I don't have any knowledge about this job, but…" となります。よほど日本的な言い方に精通していない限り、この表現は相手を混乱させてしまうでしょう。代わりに、自分の経験をフルに活用するとか、これから勉強していきたい、とかいった前向きな態度を示すような言い方を心がけましょう。"I'm looking forward to using my skills in marketing research to be as much of an asset as possible." とか "I am very excited about the opportunity to learn as much as I can in this new position." なら、相手にしっかり伝わると思います。

同様に、「どうぞよろしくお願いいたします」を "Please take care of me." とやってしまうと相手は首をかしげてしまいます。"I'm looking forward to getting to know each and every one of you." とか "I am very enthusiastic about the many new and exciting challenges that this job will present." で言い換えましょう。

POINT ❷
名前の紹介の仕方

(渡辺恵子さんが)「渡辺と申します」を "I'm Watanabe." とすると、相手は「渡辺」をファーストネーム(恵子)と思ってしまいがちです。自己紹介するときには、"Hi. I'm Keiko." だけで充分です。スピーチの場合には、"I'm Keiko Watanabe." のほうがいいでしょう。

TOPIC 1 新入社員の自己紹介

TOPIC 2 後任者の紹介
——インフォーマル（くだけたスタイルで）

長谷川里香さんはアドベント・バンクのシンガポール支店から日本へ転勤となります。後任者を連れて、これから関わっていく部署に彼女を紹介して回ります。

Track 2

Good morning Mike, Wen and Mei Ling. Do you have a minute? I'm sure that you've already heard that I'm being transferred back to the Osaka office in two weeks. My replacement arrived yesterday, so I'd like to introduce her if you don't mind.

This is Li Ming Chen. She will be taking over for me as technical manager for the office. She arrived yesterday from Shanghai. She's been with Advent for six years now and has been working as a technical advisor in Shanghai since last year. She grew up in China, but she has spent a lot of time living in Canada and Japan, so besides Chinese she speaks excellent English and Japanese.

We'll be working together for the next two weeks until I leave so that I can show her the ropes and get her up to speed on things. Please don't hesitate to send any technical or systems questions her way as they come up. She'll be in the office next to mine until I leave. After that you can find her where I sit now. Her extension will be the same as mine.

I've really enjoyed my time here over the past two years. You've been a great group to work with and I hope that we'll have the chance to work together again before too long. Thanks.

解説

Introduction

後任者を紹介する

Good morning Mike, Wen and Mei Ling(同僚の名前). Do you have a minute? I'm sure that you've already heard that I'm being transferred back to the Osaka(支店名) office in two weeks(退任時期). My replacement arrived yesterday, so I'd like to introduce her(後任者) if you don't mind.

> **訳** おはよう、マイク、ウェン、メイ・リン。ちょっといいかしら？ すでに聞いていると思うけど、私、2週間後には大阪支店に戻ることになるの。後任者が昨日こちらに着いたので、よかったら紹介したいのだけれど。

> **Notes**
> - Do you have a minute? 「1分あるかい？」が文字通りの意味だが、「ちょっと時間をくれない？」という意味の決まり文句。Do you have a sec(ond)? とも言う。
> - be transferred back to … 「～に戻る」
> - replacement 「後任者」

Body 1

後任者の略歴の紹介

This is Li Ming Chen(後任者の名前). She will be taking over for me as technical manager(役職) for the office. She arrived yesterday(到着時期) from Shanghai(前任地). She's been with Advent(会社名) for six years(就業年数) now and has been working as a technical advisor(役職) in Shanghai(勤務地) since last year. She grew up in China(育った地名), but she has spent a lot of time living in Canada and Japan(国名), so besides Chinese(母語) she speaks excellent English and Japanese(話せる言語).

> **訳** こちらがリ・ミン・チェンさん。この支店の技術担当部長として私の代わりを務めることになるの。昨日上海から到着したばかり。アドベントでは6年働いていて、去年から上海支店でテクニカル・アドバイザーをしていたわ。中国で生まれ育ったんだけど、カナダや日本にも長いこと住んでいたから、中国語のほかに英語と日本語も流暢に話すのよ。

> **Notes**
> - 後任者を紹介する公式
>   (後任者) will take over for me as (役職) for (部署)
>   She will take over for me as technical manager for the office.
> - 「雇用状態にある」という意味をwithの1語で表わすことが多い。
>   She's been with Advent for six years.
> - grow up in … 「～で育つ」

TOPIC 2 後任者の紹介——インフォーマル（くだけたスタイルで）

TOPIC 2

Body 2
引継ぎの説明

We'll be working together for the next two weeks(引継ぎ期間) until I leave so that I can show her the ropes and get her up to speed on things. Please don't hesitate to send any technical or systems(分野) questions her way as they come up. She'll be in the office next to mine until I leave. After that you can find her where I sit now. Her extension will be the same as mine.

訳 これから2週間、私が大阪に戻るまで私たちは一緒に仕事をしていきます。その間に彼女にいろいろ引継ぎができるし、仕事にも早く慣れてもらえると思うから。テクニカルな質問やシステムについての疑問点があったらどんどん彼女に聞いてね。私が移動するまでは私の隣が彼女の仕事場になります。私がいなくなったら、私の席に彼女が座ることになるんだけど。彼女の内線は私のと同じよ。

Notes
- I can show her the ropes and get her up to speed on things. は、引継ぎへの協力を行なう意思が比喩も交えてよく説明されている。
- Please don't hesitate to … 「遠慮せず〜してください」
- send 物 one's way 「(人)に物を送る」
- extension 「電話の内線番号」

Conclusion
感謝と今後への期待

I've really enjoyed my time here over the past two years(一緒に働いた年数). You've been a great group to work with and I hope that we'll have the chance to work together again before too long. Thanks.

訳 この2年間本当に楽しかったわ。こんなに素晴らしい仲間と働くことができて。近い将来、また一緒に仕事ができたらいいわね。今までありがとう。

Notes
- このパラグラフは汎用で使えるので、そのまま覚えておきたい。
- before too long 「近々」

TOPIC 3 後任者の紹介
——フォーマル（あらたまったスタイルで）

長谷川里香さんはアドベント・バンクのシンガポール支店から日本に帰国になります。会社の全体会議で後任者の紹介をします。

Track 3

Good morning. As many of you now know, I will be returning to the Osaka office tomorrow after two years here in Singapore. I would like to take this opportunity to introduce my successor, Li Ming Chen.

Ms. Chen will be assuming the position of technical manager for the Singapore office of Advent Bank. She moved here two weeks ago from Shanghai. This is her sixth year with Advent and she has been working in the position of technical advisor in Shanghai since last year. She was raised and educated in China, though she has also lived for extended periods of time in Canada and Japan. Thus, in addition to Chinese, she speaks excellent English and Japanese.

She has been shadowing me for the past two weeks, so she is now quite familiar with the duties she will be performing here. Please do not hesitate to direct any technical or systems questions to her as they arise. She will be more than pleased to assist you. Her office and extension are the same as mine.

I have truly enjoyed my time here during the past two years. It has been a pleasure working with you all and I hope that our paths will cross again in the near future. Thank you.

解説

TOPIC 3 後任者の紹介 —— フォーマル（あらたまったスタイルで）

Introduction

後任者を紹介する

Good morning. As many of you now know, I will be returning to the Osaka(新たな勤務地) office tomorrow after two years here in Singapore(これまでの勤務地). I would like to take this opportunity to introduce my successor, Li Ming Chen(後任者の名前).

訳 おはようございます。ここにいらっしゃる多くの皆さんがすでにご存知のように、私は2年間のシンガポール勤務を終え、明日、大阪支店に戻ることになりました。この席をお借りして、私の後任者、リ・ミン・チェンさんをご紹介します。

Notes
- successor（← replacement）「交代要員」から「後任者」へ。単語単位でも、くだけた調子の前トピックよりフォーマルな表現が使われていることがわかる。

Body 1

後任者の略歴の紹介

Ms. Chen(後任者の名前) will be assuming the position of technical manager(役職) for the Singapore office of Advent Bank(会社名). She moved here two weeks(引っ越し後の期間) ago from Shanghai(前任地). This is her sixth year(就業年数) with Advent(会社名) and she has been working in the position of technical advisor(役職) in Shanghai(勤務地) since last year(役職に就いた年数). She was raised and educated in China(育った地名), though she has also lived for extended periods of time in Canada and Japan(国名). Thus, in addition to Chinese(母語), she speaks excellent English and Japanese(話せる言語).

訳 チェンさんはアドベント・バンクのシンガポール支店で、テクニカル・マネジャーとして働いていただくことになります。チェンさんは2週間前に上海からこちらに引っ越してきました。アドベントで仕事を始めて6年になります。昨年からは上海支店でテクニカル・アドバイザーとして働いていらっしゃいます。中国で育ち、教育も受けていらっしゃいますが、カナダと日本にも長いことお住まいでした。ですから、中国語の他に、流暢な英語と日本語もお話しになります。

Notes
- assume the position 「任務に就く」
- This is *one's* sixth year with 会社名 「(人)が○○会社に勤めて6年になる」
- extended periods of time 「長い間」

Body 2
引継ぎの説明

She has been shadowing me for the past two weeks(引継ぎ期間), so she is now quite familiar with the duties she will be performing here. Please do not hesitate to direct any technical or systems(分野) questions to her as they arise. She will be more than pleased to assist you. Her office and extension are the same as mine.

> **訳** この2週間、私について仕事を覚えてもらっていましたので、新しい仕事にはもうずいぶん慣れました。テクニカルな、またはシステムに関する質問がありましたら、なんでも彼女に聞いてください。喜んで教えてくれると思います。彼女の部屋と内線は私が使っていたものと同じです。

> **Notes**
> - shadow　前任者または経験のある人物が仕事する様子を観察することでトレーニングする技法。英語学習にも取り入れられており、英語の音源をそっくり真似ることで、リスニング、スピーキングに役立てようとする方法はよく知られている。
> - be familiar with the duties　「仕事に精通する」
> - direct questions to …　「～に質問する」
> - be more than pleased to …　「喜んで～する」

Conclusion
感謝と今後への期待

I have truly enjoyed my time here during the past two years(就業年数). It has been a pleasure working with you all and I hope that our paths will cross again in the near future. Thank you.

> **訳** ここでの2年間、本当に楽しかったです。皆さんと一緒に仕事をすることができて光栄でした。また近い将来、何かの機会にご一緒できますことを祈っております。ありがとうございました。

> **Notes**
> - our paths will cross again　「道がまた交差する」。つまり、「またどこかで会う」ということ。

TOPIC 3 後任者の紹介——フォーマル（あらたまったスタイルで）

TOPIC 4　新入社員を歓迎する

メーカーの製造部長が東京本社にて新入社員を歓迎します。

Track 4

Good morning. On behalf of upper management, I would like to welcome you to Steelworks Manufacturing. As you are well aware, you will spend the next six months training with us here in Tokyo before going to different parts of the globe to work as product managers at our production facilities.

During your training, you will hear three key words over and over again: consistency, quality and efficiency. These concepts form the pillars of our manufacturing philosophy. We strive to produce the highest quality products as efficiently as possible with complete consistency worldwide. In other words, a product manufactured at our plant in Mexico City should be identical to the same product produced at our plant in Manila. Your jobs will be to ensure that we efficiently achieve this level of consistency at our various plants throughout the world, while meeting our high standards of quality.

We are counting on you to apply yourselves as diligently as possible during your training over the next six months. I wish you the best of luck and look forward to working with you all.

解説

Introduction

研修の始めの挨拶に使える

Good morning. On behalf of upper management, I would like to welcome you to Steelworks Manufacturing(会社名). As you are well aware, you will spend the next six months(研修期間) training with us here in Tokyo(研修地) before going to different parts of the globe to work as product managers(役職) at our production facilities.

訳 おはようございます。役員を代表しまして、スティールワークス・マニュファクチャリングへ入社されましたことを歓迎いたします。すでにご承知のとおり、皆さんはこれから半年のあいだ、この東京で我々と研修を受けていただき、その後、世界中に広がるわが社の工場の製造部長として赴任していただきます。

Notes
- on behalf of … 「〜を代表して」。スピーチの決まり文句として覚えておきたい。
- upper management 「役員」。lower managementは部長以下のクラス。

Body

研修の中心概念を説明する → 「3つ」に注意

During your training, you will hear three key words over and over again: consistency, quality and efficiency. These concepts form the pillars of our manufacturing(業務名) philosophy. We strive to produce the highest quality products as efficiently as possible with complete consistency worldwide. In other words, a product manufactured at our plant in Mexico City(都市名) should be identical to the same product produced at our plant in Manila(都市名). Your jobs will be to ensure that we efficiently achieve this level of consistency at our various plants throughout the world, while meeting our high standards of quality.

訳 研修のあいだ、次の3つのキーワードを何度も耳にされると思います。一貫性、品質、そして効率、ということばです。これら3つの概念はわが社の製造哲学の柱となっております。私たちはどの国においても一貫して最高の品質の製品を効率よく生産することに日々励んでおります。つまり、メキシコ・シティの工場で作られた製品はマニラ工場で作られたものとまったく同じである、ということです。皆さんの仕事は、わが社の製品の高品質レベルを保ちつつ、世界中どの工場においても効率よくこの一貫性を確保していただくことにあります。

TOPIC 4 新入社員を歓迎する

TOPIC 4 新入社員を歓迎する

Notes
- Bodyで説明されているのは、3つのキーワード。「3」はスピーチ英語でもっとも好まれる数字。Introduction → Body → Conclusionは3つの構成となる。1つのパラグラフの項目数も3つのことがとても多い。実際、それ以上は覚えられないからでもある。
- 最後の文章には、3つのキーワードについて関連性が明確に説明されている。
- "quality"は常に求められるビジネス要件の1つ。TQC = Total Quality Control（総合的品質管理）、QA = Quality Assurance（品質保証）などはご存知のとおり。
- form the pillars of …　「〜の柱となる」
- strive to …　「〜するよう励む」
- be identical to …　「〜と同等の」
- meet standards of quality　「品質水準を満たす」

Conclusion
健闘を祈る

We are counting on you to apply yourselves as diligently as possible during your training over the next six months（研修期間）. I wish you the best of luck and look forward to working with you all.

訳　これから半年の研修期間中、皆さまにおかれましては、いろいろと学んで努力していただけるよう期待しております。それでは頑張ってください。皆さんと共に働けることを楽しみにしております。

Notes
- count on 人　「（人）に期待する」。countは「数える」という意味だが、前置詞onが付けば、たちどころにその意味を変える。
- 第2文（I wish you …）はどのような場面にも使えるので、ぜひ暗記したい。

TOPIC 5

日本へようこそ!
――歓迎のスピーチ

研修所を訪問中のアメリカ人技術研修生に向けた歓迎スピーチです。

Track 5

Good morning and welcome to Japan. My name is Kenji Kodama, Director of the Technical Training Division. I will be overseeing your training program here in Yokohama. I know that for many of you, this is your first time to visit Japan. I hope that you will have a very productive stay and also find time to explore the rich culture and history of our country.

Let me begin with a brief overview of our schedule. We will meet here every morning at 9 a.m. The morning sessions will be used for classroom instruction. We will break for lunch at noon and reconvene at 1 p.m. The afternoon sessions will be conducted on the factory floor where you will receive hands-on training on the new production equipment.

I want your stay to be as successful and comfortable as possible, so please do not hesitate to contact me at any time if you have questions or concerns. Also, you will find my cell phone number in your welcome packets. Please use this number to get in touch with me after business hours in case of an emergency.

Again, I would like to offer a warm welcome to you all and I wish you a pleasant and productive training program.

解説

Introduction

歓迎する

Good morning and welcome to Japan. My name is Kenji Kodama, Director of the Technical Training Division(名前、役職、部門). I will be overseeing your training program here in Yokohama(研修所の所在地). I know that for many of you, this is your first time to visit Japan. I hope that you will have a very productive stay and also find time to explore the rich culture and history of our country.

> **訳** おはようございます。日本へよくいらっしゃいました。私は技術研修部長の児玉賢治と申します。ここ横浜での皆さんの研修全般をお世話させていただきます。日本へいらっしゃるのが初めてという方が多いと思いますが、どうか、この研修が実りの多いものでありますよう、また、研修中に時間を見つけてわが国の豊かな文化と歴史に触れられますよう願っております。

> **Notes**
> - oversee your training program 「研修を担当する」。つづりが似た単語に overseas があるが、こちらは「海外の」という意味。
> - "productive" は成功の指標の1つとして、ビジネスでは多用される。
> - explore 「探険する」

Body 1

予定を説明する → 司会の英語に使える！

Let me begin with a brief overview of our schedule. We will meet here every morning at 9 a.m.(研修開始時刻) The morning sessions will be used for classroom instruction(研修内容). We will break for lunch at noon(昼食開始時刻) and reconvene at 1 p.m.(午後の研修開始時刻) The afternoon sessions will be conducted on the factory floor(午後の研修場所) where you will receive hands-on training on the new production equipment.

> **訳** さてそれでは、簡単にスケジュールの確認をいたします。これから毎朝9時にここに集合してください。午前中の研修は教室で行ないます。12時から昼食をとっていただき、午後1時にまたお集まりください。午後の研修は工場にて行なわれます。新しい製造機器の使い方などを実際に使って覚えていってください。

> **Notes**
> - このパラグラフは、次のパターンの説明にぴったり。
>   集合場所と時間 → 午前の部、研修内容の紹介 → 昼食 → 集合場所と時間 → 研修内容の紹介
> - a brief overview 「簡単な概要」

- break for lunch 「昼食休憩をとる」
- reconvene at … 「〜時に再開する」
- hands-on training 「実地訓練」。カタカナではよく聞くが、つづりは大丈夫だろうか。

Body 2
成功を祈る、連絡先を知らせておく

I want your stay to be as successful and comfortable as possible, so please do not hesitate to contact me at any time if you have questions or concerns. Also, you will find my cell phone number in your welcome packets. Please use this number to get in touch with me after business hours in case of an emergency.

> [訳] 皆さんが滞在中に不自由なく成功を収められますよう、何かご質問や気になる点がありましたら、どうぞ遠慮なく私までご連絡ください。また、私の携帯電話の番号がお手元のウェルカム・パケットに記してありますので、営業時間外で緊急に連絡を取りたい場合にはその番号に電話をしてください。

> [Notes]
> - このパラグラフは、成功を祈るときの表現として汎用的に使える。
> - Do not hesitate to … 「〜することを躊躇しないでください」→「積極的に〜してください」
> - cell phone ＝「携帯電話」だが、cellular phone が本来の表現。
> - business hours 「営業時間」
> - in case of an emergency 「緊急の場合」

Conclusion
歓迎の意を表わし、成功を祈る

Again, I would like to offer a warm welcome to you all and I wish you a pleasant and productive training program(研修名).

> [訳] それでは、皆さんの研修が快適で実り多きものになりますよう心からお祈りいたしまして、歓迎のことばとさせていただきます。

> [Notes]
> - 定型文として覚えておきたい。
> - offer a warm welcome to you … ここは Welcome to … だと、歓迎の挨拶の始めのことばだが、挨拶の締めだと、この例のように welcome を offer と組み合わせて使うこともできる。もちろん、始めのことばにも使える表現。

- 「～ wish ＋人＋事」の構文（～が人の…を願う）
  We wish you a merry Christmas.
  I wish you a pleasant program.

> POINT
ビジネスばかりが能ではない！
ビジネスとプライベートを両立させるのが、英語圏で頻繁に見られる考え方です。日本では、差し詰め「文武両道」に相当するでしょう。研修に参加するだけがビジネスではありません。合間を縫って、息抜きを作るのも仕事、プライベートの両面で"productive"となる秘訣です。

TOPIC 6 工場見学
――始めの挨拶

日本のパソコンメーカーの代表団が中国のボタンとスイッチの供給先を訪問しています。中国側の製造部長がこれから見てもらう工場ツアーについて説明します。

Track 6

Good afternoon. I'd like to give you an overview of what you will see on the tour before we actually go down to the production floor.

The overall production process is divided into three main areas: molding, printing and packaging. The molding area is where the plastic is poured into molds that create the shape of the switches and buttons we produce. In the printing area, the products are painted and the button labels are printed on the face of the buttons. In the packaging area, the products are sorted into sets, wrapped and then boxed for shipping.

We operate on a two-shift schedule with shifts beginning at 7 a.m. and 3 p.m. We are in operation 16 hours per day. There is also a night crew that comes in at 11 p.m. for several hours to clean the equipment and perform any necessary maintenance.

We have about 200 employees working on each shift. We have a rotating schedule where each employee works two day shifts, two evening shifts and then has two days off.

Let me stop here for now to answer any questions you have so far.

解説

Introduction
始めのことば

Good afternoon. I'd like to give you an overview of what you will see on the tour before we actually go down to the production floor(見学場所).

訳 こんにちは。これから実際に工場の中を見学していただきますが、その前に皆さんにご覧いただくものについて簡単に説明させていただきます。

Notes
- 始めのことばの基本形：Good morning [afternoon / evening]. I would like to give you an overview of … 「〜に関する概要を説明する」

Body 1
生産工程の説明

The overall production process is divided into three main areas: molding, printing and packaging(作業工程の名称). The molding area is where the plastic is poured into molds that create the shape of the switches and buttons we produce. In the printing area, the products are painted and the button labels are printed on the face of the buttons. In the packaging area, the products are sorted into sets, wrapped and then boxed for shipping.

訳 生産工程を大きく分けると3つあります。成形、印刷、そして梱包です。成形部門ではプラスチックが鋳型に流し入れられ、スイッチやボタンの形が作られます。印刷部門では、製品の色を付けたり、ボタンの表面に付くラベルの印刷をします。梱包部門では種類別に商品がまとめられ、梱包されてから発送されます。

Notes
- 工程が3つに分割でき、それぞれの工程でどのような作業が行なわれるかについて説明している。汎用的な内容とは限らないので、作業の流れをどのように説明しているか参考にしてほしい。
- be divided into … 「〜に分けられる」
- be sorted into … 「〜にまとめられる」

Body 2
シフト制について

We operate on a two-shift schedule with shifts beginning at 7 a.m. and 3 p.m.(シフト開始時刻) We are in operation 16 hours(勤務時間) per day. There is also a night crew that comes in at 11 p.m.(夜勤開始時刻) for several hours to clean the equipment and perform any necessary maintenance.

| 訳 | この工場では午前7時と午後3時から始まる2シフト制となっております。一日に16時間操業しています。さらに午後11時から数時間、夜間に来て機械の掃除や必要なメンテナンスをする従業員もおります。 |

| Notes | • 勤務体制についての説明。工場なので、シフト制、夜勤の説明になっている。
• We operate on a two-shift schedule. 「2シフト体制が組まれている」
• night crew 「夜勤する者」
• perform any necessary maintenance 「必要なメンテナンスを行なう」
• maintain（維持する）の名詞形 maintenance は、スペリングがむずかしいので、おさえておきたい。 |

Body 3

シフト制について（続き）

We have about 200(従業員数) employees working on each shift. We have a rotating schedule where each employee works two(昼間のシフト日数) day shifts, two (夜のシフト日数) evening shifts and then has two(休みの日数) days off.

| 訳 | 午前、午後のシフトで働く従業員はそれぞれ約200人おります。各人2日の日昼のシフト、2日の夕方のシフトをこなし、2日間の休日をとるローテーションを組んでいます。 |

| Notes | • work on … shift 「〜シフトで勤務する」
• have two days off 「2日間休暇をとる」 |

Conclusion

質問をうながす

Let me stop here for now to answer any questions you have so far.

| 訳 | ここまでで、何かご質問があれば、お答えいたしますので、ここで一旦説明を区切らせていただきます。 |

| Notes | • 日本語では「質問に答える」と言うので、英語でついanswer to any questionsと"to"を付けがちだが、それは誤りである。
• so far 「ここまでで」 |

TOPIC 7 送別会のスピーチ
――転任者の送別

長谷川里香さんはアドベント・バンクのシンガポール支店から日本への転任が決まりました。送別会で長谷川さんの上司がスピーチをします。

Track 7

While I truly love meeting new people, I never enjoy having to say goodbye. This is certainly the case today as we bid farewell to our dear colleague, Rika Hasegawa.

Rika joined us from the home office in Osaka two years ago. I think it is safe to say that each and every one of us has come to rely heavily on her technical know-how. Her expertise and skill have kept the technology that we rely so heavily upon up and running around the clock. She has pulled us out of many precarious situations and has saved the day on multiple occasions. I cannot even begin to express my gratitude for her dedication and hard work.

I remember once when a number of us were working on a very time-sensitive project and the network crashed at 3 a.m. We hesitated, but knew that we had no choice but to call Rika. Not only did she know that the network was down but she was already on her way into the office to resolve the problem.

I can only say that those who will be working with Rika in her next position are indeed lucky. I do hope that they come to appreciate you as much as we have. Thank you from the bottoms of our hearts, and we wish you the best of luck.

解説

Introduction
転任者の紹介

While I truly love meeting new people, I never enjoy having to say goodbye. This is certainly the case today as we bid farewell to our dear colleague, Rika Hasegawa(転任者の名前).

> 訳　新しい人に出会うのは大好きですが、さようならを言うのはいつになっても好きになれません。今日、このように我々の仲間である長谷川里香さんを送り出さなければならないのがまさにこのことです。

> Notes
> - 第1文（While I truly love … ）はなかなかしゃれた文章となっている。覚えて使ってみたい。
> - bid farewell to …　「〜にお別れを告げる」
> - dear colleague　「親愛なる同僚」。colleagueとcollege（大学）のつづりを混同しないように。

Body 1
転任者の功績について

Rika(転任者の名前) joined us from the home office in Osaka(支店名) two years(就任期間) ago. I think it is safe to say that each and every one of us has come to rely heavily on her technical(分野) know-how. Her expertise and skill have kept the technology that we rely so heavily upon up and running around the clock. She has pulled us out of many precarious situations and has saved the day on multiple occasions. I cannot even begin to express my gratitude for her dedication and hard work.

> 訳　長谷川さんは2年前大阪本店からここに転勤になりました。長谷川さんの技術的なノウハウを、私たち一人ひとりがどれだけ頼りにしていたかわかりません。私たちがとても頼りにしていた長谷川さんの経験と能力のお陰で、会社のテクノロジーは常に正しく作動していました。いくつもの危機的な状況を気づかせてくれて、さまざまな状況において救ってくれました。彼女のこれまでの仕事ぶりには本当になんと感謝したらいいかわかりません。

> Notes
> - 技術面についての転任者の功績について説明している：rely on, expertise, skill, pull us out of many precarious situations, save the day, gratitudeがキーワードになっている。

- it is safe to say that … 「〜としてもいいでしょう」
- expertise 「専門的な経験」
- up and running 「動いている」
- around the clock 「いつも」
- pull us out 「引っぱり出す」。ここでは「助け出す」という意味。
- save the day 「救う」
- I cannot even begin to … 「〜し始めることもできない」。ここでは、感謝の意を表し（express my gratitude）始めることもできない、つまり、「とても感謝している」という意味。
- dedication 「貢献」

Body 2
転任者についてのエピソード紹介

I remember once when a number of us were working on a very time-sensitive project and the network crashed at 3 a.m. We hesitated, but knew that we had no choice but to call Rika（転任者の名前）. Not only did she know that the network was down but she was already on her way into the office to resolve the problem.

訳 一度こんなことがありました。締め切りの厳しいプロジェクトの最中、夜中の3時にネットワーク障害が起こったのです。どうしようかと迷ったのですが、長谷川さんを呼ぶしかないとだれもが思いました。そのとき、彼女はすでにネットワーク障害について情報を得ていただけでなく、問題解決のために会社に向かっているところでした。

Notes
- ちょっとしたエピソードは、その人柄を伝えるだけでなく、会社やプロジェクトにいかに貢献したかを理解させるのにとても効果的。このパラグラフでは、転任者がいかに重要な役割を果たしていたかを、ネットワークトラブルという事例を使って紹介している。
- work on … 「〜に従事する」
- time-sensitive 「時間との勝負が求められる」
- network crashed 「ネットワークが障害を起こす」
- have no choice but to … 「〜する以外方法がない」
- on *one's* way (in)to … 「〜に向かう」

Conclusion

お別れの挨拶

I can only say that those who will be working with Rika(転任者の名前) in her next position are indeed lucky. I do hope that they come to appreciate you as much as we have. Thank you from the bottoms of our hearts, and we wish you the best of luck.

訳 長谷川さんの次の職場で一緒に働ける人たちは本当に幸せです。ここにいる私たち同様、あなたに感謝するでしょう。私たちはあなたがしてくれたことに心から感謝します。どうかこれからもお幸せに。

Notes
- 締めの決まり文句は、すんなり口をついて出るように練習したい。
- Rika in her next positionとは、「次のポジションにつく里香」つまり「次の職場で」ということ。
- Thank you from the bottoms of our hearts.「心から感謝申し上げます」
- We wish you the best of luck.「今後のご活躍をお祈り申し上げます」

TOPIC 7 送別会のスピーチ――転任者の送別

TOPIC 8 会社の創立記念
──ひと言挨拶

ビデオゲーム・ソフトウェア会社の米国支社長が、年次株主総会で米国でのビジネスの15周年記念を祝ってひと言挨拶をします。

Track 8

It was on this day 15 years ago that Game Play opened its doors for business in the U.S. The video game industry was not nearly as developed then as it is today, and we were all but unknown to most consumers in the U.S. It was an uphill battle, but we stuck it out and made our best effort. Our big break came in 1996 with the release of the Titan Combat Warriors series, which was a huge hit in the U.S. This allowed us to finally achieve the brand recognition we were after.

In the past few years, the video game industry in the U.S. has taken off with the introduction of several new consoles, followed by the more recent creation of the cell phone game market. I am proud to say that despite the growing number of competitors, we have been able to maintain consistent growth since 1996.

None of this would have been possible without the steadfast loyalty of our employees, the wisdom of our board of directors and the unwavering confidence of our shareholders. We ask for your continued support over the next 15 years as we strive for even higher levels of success. Thank you.

解説

Introduction

社歴を紹介する

It was on this day 15(創業年数) years ago that Game Play(会社名) opened its doors for business in the U.S.(ターゲット市場) The video game(業界名) industry was not nearly as developed then as it is today, and we were all but unknown to most consumers in the U.S.(ターゲット市場) It was an uphill battle, but we stuck it out and made our best effort. Our big break came in 1996(繁栄が起こった年) with the release of the Titan Combat Warriors(製品シリーズ名) series, which was a huge hit in the U.S.(ターゲット市場) This allowed us to finally achieve the brand recognition we were after.

訳 15年前の今日、ゲーム・プレイ社は米国市場でのビジネスを開始しました。まだビデオゲーム産業が今ほど栄えていなかったので、わが社の名は米国ではほとんど知られていませんでした。とても厳しい状況の中、我々はよく辛抱し、またよく頑張りました。1996年に出たタイタン・コンバット・ウォーリアー・シリーズが米国で大ヒットしたおかげで、わが社名も人々に知れ渡るようになったわけです。

Notes
- 次のような流れで社歴が紹介されている：創立（opened its doors）→ 創立時の業況（not nearly as developed then as it is today）→ 努力した甲斐もあって（made our best effort）転機が訪れる（big break came）→ 業界に名を馳せる（achieve the brand recognition）
- uphill battle 「厳しい状況」
- stick it out 「辛抱する」
- we were after 「追い求めていた」

Body

ここ数年の業況と会社業績

In the past few years, the video game(業界名) industry in the U.S.(ターゲット市場) has taken off with the introduction of several new consoles, followed by the more recent creation of the cell phone game market. I am proud to say that despite the growing number of competitors, we have been able to maintain consistent growth since 1996(繁栄が起こった年).

訳 ここ数年、米国のビデオゲーム業界はさまざまな新しいコンソールの発売で好調となり、それが最近の携帯電話ゲーム市場での開発につながっています。競争相手の増加にも関わらず、1996年以来、わが社がこうして成長を続けていることを誇りに思います。

TOPIC 8　会社の創立記念――ひと言挨拶

TOPIC 8 会社の創立記念──ひと言挨拶

Notes
- take off 「離陸する」。つまり、好調となる様子を「軌道に乗る」と描写した表現。頻繁に使われる。
- console 「ディスプレイ画面」
- I am proud to say that … 会社の業績を称えることは、英語のスピーチでは普通です。
- competitors 「競合他社」
- maintain consistent growth 「一貫して成長を遂げる」

Conclusion
従業員にお礼を言う

None of this would have been possible without the steadfast loyalty of our employees, the wisdom of our board of directors and the unwavering confidence of our shareholders. We ask for your continued support over the next 15 years as we strive for even higher levels of success. Thank you.

訳　これも、日々会社のために働いてくれる従業員、賢明な役員、そして何より変わらぬ信頼をおいてくださる株主の皆さまのお陰と心より思っております。これからの15年もまたさらなる成功をおさめてまいりますので、どうぞ引き続きご支援、ご鞭撻のほど、よろしくお願い申し上げます。ありがとうございました。

Notes
- このパラグラフは、会社の役員（社長）が、従業員を始め関係者にお礼を言う際に最適。余裕があれば、パラグラフごと覚えて活用したい。
- steadfast loyalty 「日々の忠誠」
- board of directors 「役員」
- unwavering confidence 「変わらぬ信頼」
- shareholders 「株主」。stakeholdersが対比で使われる。
- ask for … 「〜をお願いする」

> **POINT**
> ### 自慢も我慢!?
> 英語でのスピーチでは日本語でのスピーチに比べ、"自己賞賛"の表現が多くなりがちです。会社の創立記念に際してのスピーチでもこれはいえます。会社の業績をすべて挙げ、それに貢献した人たちにお礼を言うのです。この例でも最後のパラグラフではお礼となっています。

TOPIC 9 忘年会でのスピーチ

国際的なグラフィックデザイン会社の社長が、会社の忘年会で開会の挨拶をします。

Track 9

Good evening, everybody. It's great to see so many friendly faces here tonight.

It has been a wonderful year for us here at Grafix International. Our third quarter sales jumped by 34%, our biggest increase to date. We have also been able to expand the number of employees on the design teams and sales force by 25% this year. Our family has grown to now include over 100 members. This is truly something to be proud of.

We have had to face a number of hurdles throughout 2005. Some of these challenges included increased competition and a stagnant economy. Nonetheless, the collective efforts of each and every person in this room have prevailed to give us our best year yet. I would like to thank all of you for a job well done.

There is no doubt that next year will surely present new obstacles to overcome. I have the utmost confidence that as a team we can work together to succeed in any situation, so I ask for your perseverance and determination to make 2006 an amazing year! Thank you.

解説

Introduction

挨拶、参加への感謝

Good evening, everybody. It's great to see so many friendly faces here tonight.

> 訳　こんばんは、皆さん。今日はこのように多くの親しい方々にお集まりいただいて、とてもうれしいです。

> Notes
> - see many friendly faces　直訳すると「親しい顔を見る」だが、see は「会う」という意味。see many new facesと言えば、「多くの人に会う」ということ。

Body 1

四半期業績の説明

It has been a wonderful year for us here at Grafix International(会社名). Our third(四半期名) quarter sales jumped by 34(売上高の伸び率)%, our biggest increase to date. We have also been able to expand the number of employees on the design(チーム名) teams and sales force by 25(デザインチームと販売員の増加率)% this year. Our family has grown to now include over 100(従業員数) members. This is truly something to be proud of.

> 訳　今年はグラフィックス・インターナショナル社にとってとてもいい年でした。第3四半期の売上げ増が34%を記録しましたが、これは今まででいちばんの伸び率です。また、今年はデザイン・チームと営業に新しい仲間が増え、25%の従業員増となり、いまや、わが社は100人以上の大所帯です。これは本当に素晴らしいことです。

> Notes
> - 四半期ごとの業績報告：first, second, third, fourth quarter 第1四半期～第4四半期まであるのはご存知だろう。
> - jumped by …とjumped to …の違いは大丈夫だろうか。前者は増加分、後者は増加した後の数値を指す表現。
> - to date　「本日まで」
> - expand　「拡大する」
> - sales force　「販売員」

Body 2

困難な状況を乗り越えた

We have had to face a number of hurdles throughout 2005(年度). Some of these challenges included increased competition and a stagnant economy. Nonetheless, the collective efforts of each and every person in this room have prevailed to give us our best year yet. I would like to thank all of you for a job well done.

> **訳** 今年2005年は年間を通してさまざまな困難を乗り越えてきました。これらの中には競争相手の増加や経済の低迷などがありました。しかし、ここにいらっしゃる皆さん一人ひとりの努力で、こうして最高の年にすることができました。よい仕事をしてくださってありがとうございました。

Notes
- 問題解決型のロジックは次のとおり
  問題 → 分析 → 解決策 → 成功 → 感謝
  困難な状況（hurdles）を乗り越えた → 困難な状況（increased competition and stagnant economy）の説明 → チームの力（collective efforts）が打ち克つ → それについて感謝する
- challenges　日本人がdifficultと言う場合、challengingにニュアンスがより近いことがある。
- prevail 「打ち克つ」

Conclusion

協力を依頼する

There is no doubt that next year will surely present new obstacles to overcome. I have the utmost confidence that as a team we can work together to succeed in any situation, so I ask for your perseverance and determination to make 2006(年度) an amazing year! Thank you.

> **訳** 来年もまた乗り越えなければならない新たな障害にぶつかると思いますが、みんなで力を合わせていけば、どんな状況下でも成功につなげる自信があります。どうか2006年も頑張って、素晴らしい年にしていきましょう。どうもありがとうございました。

Notes
- 問題解決型のロジック
  分析 → 解決策 → 依頼
  予想される問題（new obstacles）→ チームによる解決（work together）→ 協力の依頼（ask for …）

TOPIC 9 忘年会でのスピーチ

- There is no doubt that … 「疑いなく〜」
- utmost confidence 「この上ない自信」
- perseverance 「忍耐」
- determination 「決意」

TOPIC 10 親睦会
——花見の宴会

課長が各国から来ているスタッフに向けて花見の宴会で挨拶をします。

Track 10

Welcome! I'm really glad to see that everybody was able to make it today. As you know, this is a very special time of year in Japan. It is a season of new life, beauty and peace. The greatest beauties in life, however, usually do not last longer than the blink of an eye. For this reason, I am a true believer that we must always make time to stop and smell the roses, or the cherry blossoms in this case.

If you think about it, we spend more time together than we do with our own families. But how can we expect to work well together unless, like a family, we stop and take the time to get to know each other? This is why I think that events like this are so important. Taking the time to get to know each of your colleagues is an investment well worth making.

With that said, I would like to propose a toast to you all. May we continue to work throughout the year as one happy family. May we learn to rely on each other as needed and treat each other with respect. Thank you all for your company this evening. Enjoy the food, the drinks and most of all the beautiful scenery and people around you. Cheers!

解説

Introduction

花見参加への感謝

Welcome! I'm really glad to see that everybody was able to make it today. As you know, this is a very special time of year in Japan. It is a season of new life, beauty and peace. The greatest beauties in life, however, usually do not last longer than the blink of an eye. For this reason, I am a true believer that we must always make time to stop and smell the roses, or the cherry blossoms in this case.

訳 ようこそ！　今日は皆さんおそろいで、とてもうれしいです。ご存知のように、この時期は日本ではとても特別です。新しい生命、美、そして平和の季節です。人生における最も美しい時期は、しかし、瞬きひとつするよりも短いものです。ですから、私は心から信じるのです。私たちはいつも立ち止まってバラの香りをかぐ時間を持つべきだと。今日この日は桜ですが。

Notes
- I'm really glad to see …　「お越しいただいてとてもうれしい」。参加者に対する歓迎の気持ちを表わしている。
- make it　「参加する」
- the blink of an eye　「瞬き」。短い様を表わす比喩。
- stop and smell the roses　「立ち止まってバラの花の香りをかぐ」。つまり「ゆっくりと楽しむ、鑑賞する」。stop to … とも表現される。

Body

会の主旨を説明する

If you think about it, we spend more time together than we do with our own families. But how can we expect to work well together unless, like a family, we stop and take the time to get to know each other? This is why I think that events like this are so important. Taking the time to get to know each of your colleagues is an investment well worth making.

訳 自分の家族といるより、ここにいる仕事仲間といる時間のほうが長いですよね。でも、家族でもそうだと思いますが、ちょっと立ち止まって相手を理解する時間を持たずして、どうやって一緒にいい状態で仕事ができましょう。私がこのような席を設けるのを大切だと思っているのは、そういう理由からです。仕事仲間を知ることは大きな財産です。

Notes
- お花見をはじめとして「飲み会」といった集まりに対して、その意義を理解している人はそう多くない。そこで、従業員が集まって催す会の意義をこのパラグラフのように説明できたら素晴らしいことだ。
- get to know each other 「相手を理解する」。knowは「知っている」という状態。
- an investment well worth making 「そうすることに価値のある投資」

Conclusion

乾杯の音頭をとる

With that said, I would like to propose a toast to you all. May we continue to work throughout the year as one happy family. May we learn to rely on each other as needed and treat each other with respect. Thank you all for your company this evening. Enjoy the food, the drinks and most of all the beautiful scenery and people around you. Cheers!

訳 さてでは、ここで乾杯をいたしましょう。ひとつの幸せな家族のようにこれからも働けますように。必要に応じてお互いに頼り合うことを学び、また尊敬の念を持って付き合っていかれますように。今晩集まっていただいてありがとうございました。食事、飲み物、そして何といっても周りのこの美しい景色と仲間とのおしゃべりを楽しんでください。乾杯！

Notes
- 英語圏では、乾杯の音頭を担当する人というのはいないので、話し手がそのまま乾杯をうながしてしまってよい。例のように、I would like to propose a toast to you all. で始め、May …で健闘を祈り、Cheers! で乾杯する。
- With that said, … 「それでは」「さてでは」
- propose a toast 「乾杯する」
- treat each other with respect 「尊敬の念を持って付き合う」
- 英語には「いただきます」「ごちそうさま」という表現はない。あえて言えば、"Let's dig in." と "I'm finished (done)." がそれらに相当するだろう。

TOPIC 11 親睦会
——新年会

インターナショナル・マーケティングの取締役が新年会の挨拶をします。

Track 11

Happy New Year! Thank you all for being able to attend this evening. I hope that you had a refreshing holiday break and that each one of you is ready to put your best foot forward as we enter 2007.

You all did an excellent job this past year, and so I ask you to simply keep up the good work. We have some exciting challenges that lie ahead with the release of our new lineup of facial creams in April. And, as you know, we'll be breaking into the Thai market in July. The success of these upcoming endeavors will lie greatly on the shoulders of our division. I haven't the slightest doubt, however, that we are more than capable of pulling off anything that is asked of us. So I'll be counting on each and every one of you to give it your all.

I would like to express how truly fortunate I feel to be managing such a creative, capable and dependable team. You are all a joy to work with, and I think we have a very fun year to look forward to in 2007. For now, kick back, relax and enjoy the evening. Thank you and I wish you all a happy, healthy and successful new year!

解説

Introduction
始めのことば

Happy New Year! Thank you all for being able to attend this evening. I hope that you had a refreshing holiday break and that each one of you is ready to put your best foot forward as we enter 2007(年).

> **訳** 明けましておめでとうございます！ 今宵このようにお集まりいただき、ありがとうございます。休暇中、心身ともにリフレッシュしてこられたかと思います。2007年の始まりにあたり、皆さん一人ひとりが一所懸命、頑張ってください。

Notes
- 参加への感謝 → 正月休暇への言及
- Happy New Year!　大文字になっている点に注意。
- holiday break　ここでは「正月休暇」。holidayは「祭日」、vacationは個人でとる「休暇」。
- put *one's* best foot forward　「最高の出だしを切る」

Body
今年の予定を概観する

You all did an excellent job this past year, and so I ask you to simply keep up the good work. We have some exciting challenges that lie ahead with the release of our new lineup of facial creams (製品名) in April (予定月). And, as you know, we'll be breaking into the Thai (ターゲット市場) market in July (予定月). The success of these upcoming endeavors will lie greatly on the shoulders of our division. I haven't the slightest doubt, however, that we are more than capable of pulling off anything that is asked of us. So I'll be counting on each and every one of you to give it your all.

> **訳** 昨年は皆さん本当に素晴らしい仕事ぶりでした。私がここで申し上げたいことは、今年もそのまま良い状態を保っていただきたい、ということです。4月にはフェイシャル・クリームの新しいシリーズの発売などいくつかの大きな山場があります。さらに、7月のタイ市場への新規参入は、皆さんもご存知のとおりです。これら来るプロジェクトが実を結ぶかどうかは私たちの部署にかかっています。私たちが、期待されている以上の結果を出せるであろうことは、疑う余地はありませんが。ぜひ、一人ひとりがベストを尽くしてください。

TOPIC 11　親睦会——新年会

Notes
- 次の流れで説明がなされている： 去年の労をねぎらう（did an excellent job）→ 今年も同じ活躍を求める（keep up the good work）→ 今後の予定 → 従業員の肩にかかっている（lie on the shoulders of our division）→ それも難なくこなせるだろう（more than capable of … ）→ 期待している（I'll be counting on …）
- lie ahead 「待ち構えている」
- break into … 「〜に参入する」
- I haven't the slightest doubt that … 「疑いなく〜する」
- pull off 「結果に残す」
- give it *one's* all 「ベストを尽す」

Conclusion

感謝の意を表し、新年会を開催する

I would like to express how truly fortunate I feel to be managing such a creative, capable and dependable team. You are all a joy to work with, and I think we have a very fun year to look forward to in 2007(年). For now, kick back, relax and enjoy the evening. Thank you and I wish you all a happy, healthy and successful new year!

訳 このようなクリエイティブで、有能で、信頼のおけるチームをまとめるのは本当に幸せなことです。私は皆さんととても楽しく仕事をさせてもらっています。2007年もまた良い年にしましょう。今夜はしばらく仕事を忘れて、ゆっくりと楽しんでください。では、今年も皆さんにとって幸多き、健康な、そして成功の一年でありますように！

Notes
- チームに対する褒めことばとして、creative, competent, capable, reliable, dependable がある。チームプレイヤーであることを褒める文章として、You're great to work with. というのも頻繁に使われる。
- dependable 「信頼のおける」
- You are all a joy to work with. 直訳すると、「皆さんは、一緒に働くのにとても楽しい（喜び）」となる。意訳は **訳** を参照。
- kick back 「くつろぐ」

TOPIC 12 退職 I
――送ることば

児玉慎二さんはアドバンテージ・インターナショナル・ビジネス・ソリューションで21年間働き、退職の時を迎えようとしています。会社で退職祝いのパーティーが催されることになり、児玉さんとこの10年一緒に働いてきたジュリア・クレイマーさんが児玉さんのスピーチの前にひと言、送ることばを頼まれました。

Track 12

Good evening, everybody. I'm Julia Kramer, a senior consultant in the IT Consulting Division. Thank you all so much for attending this farewell gathering for our dear colleague, Mr. Shinji Kodama. Shinji came on board over 21 years ago in a very different time compared to today. He began as a computer programmer, stuck it out during hard times when the bubble burst, and was instrumental in changing the company's focus to internet-based IT consulting in the mid-90s. We owe much of our growth and success in Japan to Shinji's innovative ideas and bold initiatives.

I have had the honor of working with Shinji over the past ten years. He has been not only a supervisor but also a colleague, a mentor and a friend. I, as well as everybody else who has been lucky enough to work with him, will miss him dearly. It will certainly not be easy to get by without him. Anybody would have a hard time filling his shoes.

I understand that he and his wife will be relocating to Hawaii where their daughters currently reside. We're all looking forward to visiting him quite often!

Without further ado, let me now turn over the podium to our dear friend and colleague, Shinji Kodama.

解説

Introduction

話し手紹介の英語 → 人の紹介に使える！

Good evening, everybody. I'm Julia Kramer(自分の名前), a senior consultant(役職) in the IT Consulting Division(部門名). Thank you all so much for attending this farewell gathering for our dear colleague, Mr. Shinji Kodama(退職者の名前). Shinji(退職者のファースト・ネーム) came on board over 21 years(就業年数) ago in a very different time compared to today. He began as a computer programmer(当初の職種), stuck it out during hard times when the bubble burst, and was instrumental in changing the company's focus to internet-based IT consulting(分野) in the mid-90s. We owe much of our growth and success in Japan to Shinji's(退職者のファースト・ネーム) innovative ideas and bold initiatives.

訳 皆さん、こんばんは。ITコンサルティング部、シニア・コンサルタントのジュリア・クレイマーです。本日は私たちの同僚である児玉慎二さんの送別会にお集まりいただきまして、誠にありがとうございます。児玉さんは21年前に入社しましたが、その頃は今とは随分事情が違っていました。児玉さんはコンピュータ・プログラマーとして入社し、バブルがはじけ会社にとっても厳しい時期をともに耐え忍びました。その後、90年代半ばにインターネットベースのITコンサルティングへと会社が焦点を変えるのにあたり、児玉さんは多いに貢献されました。わが社の日本における発展と成功は、児玉さんの革新的なアイディアと際立ったイニシアティブに負うところが大きいと思います。

Notes
- 自分の名前・役職紹介 → 送別会参加への感謝 → 退職者の名前紹介 → 退職者の社内での履歴紹介（退職者の功績を紹介）
- come on board = join our companyという意味。
- stick it out 「耐え忍ぶ」。stuckはstickの過去形。
- be instrumental in … 「〜するのに貢献する」。カタカナで「インストルメンタル」というと、歌詞のない楽器だけによる音楽を指すので間違えないように。
- owe … to 〜 「…は〜のおかげによる」
- innovative 「革新的な」
- bold 「際立った」「大胆な」

Body 1
人柄の紹介

I have had the honor of working with Shinji(退職者のファースト・ネーム) over the past ten (期間)years. He has been not only a supervisor but also a colleague, a mentor and a friend. I, as well as everybody else who has been lucky enough to work with him(退職者), will miss him(退職者) dearly. It will certainly not be easy to get by without him(退職者). Anybody would have a hard time filling his(退職者) shoes.

訳 この10年、児玉さんと一緒に仕事をさせていただいたことをありがたく思っています。私にとって児玉さんは上司というだけではなく、同僚、恩師、また良き友でもありました。ここにお集まりの皆さん同様、私も児玉さんの退職をとても残念に思っています。児玉さんなしではいろいろな面で大変だと思います。児玉さんがやられていたことを引き継ぐのは並大抵のことではありませんから。

Notes
- have the honor of …　「〜できて光栄である」
- colleague　「同僚」。mentorは「恩師」のほかに、「指導者」にも相当する語。
- get by　「なんとかやっていく」
- fill *one's* shoes = replace *one*

Body 2
退職者の今後の予定について

I understand that he and his wife(退職者の家族) will be relocating to Hawaii(引っ越し先) where their daughters(退職者の家族) currently reside. We're all looking forward to visiting him(退職者) quite often!

訳 退職後、児玉さんは奥さまとハワイに越されることになりますが、そちらにはすでにお嬢さま方も住んでいらっしゃるということです。これからは頻繁に児玉さんにお目にかかることができるとみんなで楽しみにしています。

Notes
- relocate to … = move to …　「〜に引っ越す」
- reside = live

TOPIC 12 退職 I ── 送ることば

TOPIC 12 退職 I ── 送ることば

Conclusion
話し手の紹介に使える！

Without further ado, let me now turn over the podium to our dear friend and colleague, Shinji Kodama(退職者の名前).

訳 さて、私たちの友であり、同僚である児玉慎二さんに、こちらに来ていただきましょう。

Notes
- Without further ado, … 「さて」。話し手紹介の常套句。
- turn over the podium to 人 「演壇を人に向ける」とは「話をしてもらう」という意味で、話し手紹介の際の決まり文句。podiumは「演壇」。

POINT
気軽な英語ビジネス!?

1) ビジネスのシチュエーションにおいて、同僚（上司も）をファースト・ネームで呼ぶことはめずらしくありません。
2) 英語でのスピーチでは、ジョークやちょっとした気の利いたコメントで聴衆を笑わせることがあります。もちろん、沈鬱な場でのジョークは控えますが。

TOPIC 13 退職 II
―― 最後の挨拶

児玉慎二さんが退職祝いのパーティーで来賓に向けて話をします。たった今、同僚のジュリア・クレイマーさんより紹介を受けました。

Track 13

Thank you, Julia, for the wonderful introduction. I am touched to see that so many colleagues have turned up to bid me farewell this evening.

It was over 20 years ago that I joined Advantage. I was fortunate enough to be here just when the internet began to really take off in the 90s. This was a monumental turning point for the company as we made the decision to jump feet first into the business of internet-based consulting. In a sense, it was a leap of blind faith that involved a lot of risk. But, I am thankful that all of those working around me had the courage to stick it out through these times of uncertainty. As you all know, our efforts paid off and our courage was rewarded with great success. These were some of the most exciting years of my life, and I would not trade them for anything.

Although I am looking forward to relaxing in my retirement, I will definitely miss working with all of you. You have been like a family to me. And, like a family, we have lived through many happy as well as difficult moments together. I will treasure these memories as long as I live. Thank you.

解説

TOPIC 13 退職Ⅱ——最後の挨拶

Introduction

紹介を受けたときの返答に使える！

Thank you, Julia(紹介者の名前), for the wonderful introduction. I am touched to see that so many colleagues have turned up to bid me farewell this evening.

訳 クレイマーさん、素敵なご紹介をしていただいてありがとうございました。今晩、お別れを言いにこんなにもたくさんの皆さんがいらしてくださって感激しています。

Notes
- Thank you, Julia, for …　相手をファースト・ネームで呼ぶことは、親近感をもたらす。日本語訳と比べてみよう。
- be touched　「感激する」。類似表現に be moved がある。
- turn up　「参加する」
- bid me farewell　「お別れを言う」

Body

苦難を乗り越えた末の成功を説明する

It was over 20(就業年数) years ago that I joined Advantage(会社名). I was fortunate enough to be here just when the Internet(媒体) began to really take off in the 90s(年代). This was a monumental turning point for the company as we made the decision to jump feet first into the business of internet-based consulting(分野). In a sense, it was a leap of blind faith that involved a lot of risk. But, I am thankful that all of those working around me had the courage to stick it out through these times of uncertainty. As you all know, our efforts paid off and our courage was rewarded with great success. These were some of the most exciting years of my life, and I would not trade them for anything.

訳 私がアドバンテージ社に入社したのは20年も前のことです。90年代に本格的にインターネットが始まったとき、この会社にいられたのは本当に運が良かったと思います。インターネットベースのコンサルティング会社としての一歩を踏み出すことを決めたとき、わが社にとって記念すべき転換期となりました。ある意味では、大きな危険を伴った賭けに出たことになります。この不安定な時期にも会社にとどまる勇気を持って私の周りで働いてくださった方々に対して、心からお礼申し上げます。皆さまもご存知のように、私たちの努力と勇気は報われ、大きな成功と相成りました。あの頃は私の人生の中でも何ものにも代えられない刺激的な時期でした。

Notes
- join ABC 「ABC社に入社する」というと、enterを思いつくが、joinの方がふさわしい。enterは「入る」という動作を表わすが、joinは「加わる」「結びつく」という概念をも含む。
- take off 「離陸する」、つまり「始まる」。
- turning point 「転換期」
- jump feet first 「一歩を踏み出す」
- stick it out 「耐え忍ぶ」
- our efforts paid off 「努力が実る」
- be rewarded with … 「〜で報われる」
- trade A for B 「AをBで代える」

Conclusion
引退後について説明し、感謝で終わる

Although I am looking forward to relaxing in my retirement, I will definitely miss working with all of you. You have been like a family to me. And, like a family, we have lived through many happy as well as difficult moments together. I will treasure these memories as long as I live. Thank you.

訳　退職後のゆったりした生活を楽しみにしてはいるのですが、皆さまとともに働いた日々をきっと懐かしく思い出すでしょう。皆さまは私にとっては家族のようでしたから。家族同様、私たちは一緒に楽しいことのみならず、大変なこともいろいろ経験してきました。その数々の思い出をずっと大切にしていきたいと思っています。どうもありがとうございました。

Notes
- 企業が家族にたとえられるのは、英語でも同じ。
- in my retirement 「退職後に」
- live through … 「〜を生き抜く」「〜を経験する」
- treasure … 「〜を大切にする」

TOPIC 13　退職 II —— 最後の挨拶

TOPIC 14 激励するスピーチ I

日本の国際衣服デザイン会社の社長が多国籍スタッフに対し、現在会社が低迷状態にあることを話します。

Track 14

Good morning. By now, you've all heard our latest earnings report for the second quarter. Sales have declined again, down 7.5% compared to the same quarter last year. Sales for the year are now down 12% compared to last year at this time.

Nonetheless, I remain optimistic that this downturn is only temporary. The currency exchange market has not been in our favor since last year and the sales of clothing in North America and Europe have been stagnant. These factors, however, are expected to turn around during the second half of this year. Once this happens, our situation will improve greatly and we will be back on track.

Until then, however, I ask everybody to hang in there. Often in times like these, employees are tempted to jump ship and run for higher ground. I'm happy to report that despite the sluggish year we've had so far, we still have everybody on board. Let's keep it that way.

Keep morale up by thinking positively about the coming months. I am happy to individually address any specific concerns that come up as we work to get through this. Thank you.

解説

TOPIC 14

激励するスピーチ I

Introduction
悪い業績結果を報告する

Good morning. By now, you've all heard our latest earnings report for the second(四半期名) quarter. Sales have declined again, down 7.5(四半期別売上高増加率)% compared to the same quarter last year. Sales for the year are now down 12(通年売上高増加率)% compared to last year at this time.

訳 おはようございます。第2四半期の売上げ報告についてはすでに聞いていらっしゃると思います。去年の同四半期に比べ、7.5％の売上げ減となりました。年間の売上げは去年のこの時期と比較して12％減です。

Notes
- by now 「すでに」
- latest earnings 「最新の売上高」
- sales have declined 「売上高が減少した」。比較する対象は、前年同四半期（compared to the same quarter last year）と前年のこの時期（compared to last year at this time）である。

Body 1
今後は楽観視できるだろう

Nonetheless, I remain optimistic that this downturn is only temporary. The currency exchange market has not been in our favor since last year and the sales of clothing(商品) in North America and Europe(ターゲット市場) have been stagnant. These factors, however, are expected to turn around during the second half of this year. Once this happens, our situation will improve greatly and we will be back on track.

訳 それでも、私はこの状況がそう長くは続かないと楽観視しています。昨年から続くドル安の為替相場や北米、ヨーロッパでの衣料売り上げ停滞などの影響を受けていると思うのですが、こういったことは今年の後半ごろには好転すると予想されます。そうなれば、わが社の売上げもずいぶん良くなるでしょうし、また以前のようになります。

Notes
- remain optimistic 「楽観視する」
- downturn 「後退」
- currency exchange market 「為替相場」
- be in *one's* favor 「〜の味方である」「〜に有利である」
- turn around 「好転する」
- be back on track 「以前の状態に戻る」

Body 2

励ます

Until then, however, I ask everybody to hang in there. Often in times like these, employees are tempted to jump ship and run for higher ground. I'm happy to report that despite the sluggish year we've had so far, we still have everybody on board. Let's keep it that way.

訳 それまでは、どうか我慢してください。こういった時期には辞めてもう少し条件のいい会社に移る人も出てくるものです。今のように会社が不調の年にもかかわらず、皆さんが全員残っていてくださることをうれしく思います。これからもどうかよろしくお願いします。

Notes
- よい条件を追い求めて転職する（jump ship and run for higher ground）のではなく、我慢する（hang in there）ことを説いている。
- hang in 「我慢する」
- be tempted to … 「～するよう駆られる」
- sluggish 「不調の」
- have 人 on board　ここでは「(人が) 会社を辞めずに残っている」という意味。

Conclusion

個別面談をうながす

Keep morale up by thinking positively about the coming months. I am happy to individually address any specific concerns that come up as we work to get through this. Thank you.

訳 良くなるであろう数か月後を考えて勤労意欲を高めましょう。この時期をやり過ごすために、懸案事項が出てきたらなんでも一人ひとりにお話しします。ありがとうございました。

Notes
- スピーチだけでは、個人の悩みに対応することはできない。そこで、個人面談も積極的にする（individually address）構えを説明しておくと効果的だろう。
- keep morale up 「勤労意欲を高める」
- think positively 「プラス思考をする」
- get through … 「～をやり過ごす」

TOPIC 15 激励するスピーチ II

日本の国際的な発光ダイオード技術会社の最高責任者が、会社が告訴された特許侵害裁判について話をします。

Track 15

Five weeks ago, we were notified of a patent infringement lawsuit being filed by Lightmaker LED, one of our biggest competitors. Since then, our legal department has been working around the clock to mitigate the situation. Depositions began last week, and we are hopeful that we will be able to settle out of court. Although we are optimistic, we are not out of the woods yet.

We do not feel that Lightmaker has a legitimate claim. Nonetheless, we offered to settle as a cautious form of damage control. If our offer to settle is rejected, you can be sure that we will fight this to the bitter end. It is in times like these that a company must come together and stand as one against external threats. We can win only if we fight as a team, so I ask for you to stand behind us and offer your unwavering support.

If the case goes to trial, it could turn into a long and arduous battle. Some of you may even be asked to testify. I hope that we can count on you if and when that time comes.

For now, I ask for your patience and positive thoughts. We will keep you apprised of any major turn of events. Thank you.

解説

TOPIC 15　激励するスピーチⅡ

Introduction
特許侵害案件の状況を説明する

Five weeks ago, we were notified of a patent infringement lawsuit being filed by Lightmaker LED（訴訟を起こした会社名）, one of our biggest competitors. Since then, our legal department has been working around the clock to mitigate the situation. Depositions began last week, and we are hopeful that we will be able to settle out of court. Although we are optimistic, we are not out of the woods yet.

訳　5週間前、最も大きな競争相手の1つであるライトメーカー・発光ダイオード社がわが社に対して特許侵害の訴訟を起こしたことを知らされました。以来、法務部は状況の緩和に昼夜働いています。宣誓証言が先週始まりましたが、裁判によらずに解決できるように願っています。我々は楽観的にこの状況を捉えていますが、まだ危機から脱したわけではありません。

Notes
- グローバル化の影響で、各国がお互いの技術を参考にすることができる時代。それは、特許侵害の案件を増加させ、今では特許侵害に関わる訴訟（patent infringement lawsuit）も日常茶飯事といわれるまでになった。本案件では、和解（settle out of court）に至りそうな状況だ。
- be notified of …　「〜を知らされる」
- be filed by …　「〜により訴訟が起きる」
- legal department　「法務部」
- work around the clock　「昼夜働く」
- deposition　「宣誓証言」
- be out of the woods　「危機から脱する」

Body 1
裁判につながったケースを想定し結束をうながす

We do not feel that Lightmaker（訴訟を起こした会社名） has a legitimate claim. Nonetheless, we offered to settle as a cautious form of damage control. If our offer to settle is rejected, you can be sure that we will fight this to the bitter end. It is in times like these that a company must come together and stand as one against external threats. We can win only if we fight as a team, so I ask for you to stand behind us and offer your unwavering support.

| 訳 | ライトメーカー社が正当な特許申請をしているとは思っていません。しかし、事態の悪化を招かないように和解を申し出ました。もし和解策が拒否された場合、最後まで戦うことをご承知ください。このような時こそ、企業が一丸となって外敵に向かわなければなりません。一緒に戦ってこそ勝つことができるのです。皆さんの変わらぬご協力をお頼み申し上げます。

TOPIC 15
激励するスピーチ II

| Notes |
- 和解に至らなかった場合には、資金的にも人的にも相当の痛手を被るおそれがある。その場合には、やはりチームワーク（fight as a team）が求められる。日本でもそうだが、fightとあるとおり、裁判は戦いであり、企業の存続をかけた勝負なのである。
- legitimate 「合法的な」
- offer to settle 「和解を申し出る」
- to the bitter end 「最後まで」
- against external threats 「外敵に対して」
- stand behind 人 「（人）に協力する」

Body 2
証言を求められた場合の協力

If the case goes to trial, it could turn into a long and arduous battle. Some of you may even be asked to testify. I hope that we can count on you if and when that time comes.

| 訳 | 万が一、裁判に持ち越される場合には長く厳しい戦いとなるでしょう。皆さんの中には宣誓証言するよう依頼を受ける方が出てくるかもしれません。そのような時はどうぞよろしくお願いします。

| Notes |
- 証言を求められる（be asked to testify）こともある。count on youを勘違いしないように。これは何も企業に有利になるような偽証を期待しているわけではない。ご承知のとおり、裁判の証言では事実を述べることが前提となっている。
- go to trial 「裁判に持ち越す」
- turn into … 「～になる」

Conclusion

協力を要請する

For now, I ask for your patience and positive thoughts. We will keep you apprised of any major turn of events. Thank you.

訳　今はただ、忍耐強く、良い方向に考えるようお願いするだけです。今後の動向は追ってお知らせします。どうもありがとうございました。

Notes
- プラス思考（positive thoughts）は頻繁に使われるスキルの1つ。
- keep you apprised of … 「〜を追って知らせる」

TOPIC 16 企業概要 I
──自動車業界

自動車部品メーカーの投資家担当部長の矢野修二さんが、将来の投資家に対して簡単に会社概要を話します。

Track 16

Good morning. My name is Shuji Yano, head of Investor Relations at Auto Steer, Co. Ltd. Let me begin with a brief overview of our company.

We have been manufacturing steering wheels and accessory parts, such as turn signal handles and horn systems, since our inception in 1978. Our products are sold in Japan, as well as in China, North America and Europe. Our market share is just under 20 percent in Japan and averages between five and ten percent in our overseas markets.

We currently have two domestic production facilities in Chiba and Shizuoka prefectures. We also have overseas plants in China, Mexico and Germany. We supply steering wheels, parts and accessory components for six major automotive manufacturers worldwide. Our total annual sales in 2005 surpassed 10 billion yen. With our plans for further expansion into the Asian market, particularly in Korea, we expect a 15% increase in sales in 2006.

Allow me to stop here to entertain any questions that you have so far.

解説

Introduction
簡単な自己紹介とスピーチの目的

Good morning. My name is Shuji Yano(名前), head(役職) of Investor Relations(部署名) at Auto Steer, Co. Ltd. (企業名) Let me begin with a brief overview of our company.

訳 おはようございます。私はオート・ステア株式会社、投資家担当部長の矢野修二と申します。簡単にわが社の概要について説明させていただきます。

Notes
- 自己紹介の公式
  名前，役職 of 部署名 at 会社名
  Shuji Yano, head of Investor Relations at Auto Steer, Co. Ltd.
- overview 「概要」

Body 1
企業概要を説明する → 製品、市場シェアの報告に使える！

We have been manufacturing steering wheels and accessory parts(製品名), such as turn signal handles and horn systems, since our inception in 1978(創業年). Our products are sold in Japan(主要な市場となる国名), as well as in China, North America and Europe(その他の国名). Our market share is just under 20(市場シェア率) percent in Japan(国名) and averages between five and ten(市場シェア率) percent in our overseas markets.

訳 私どもは1978年の創業以来、自動車のハンドル、そして方向指示レバーやクラクションなどの自動車部品を製造してまいりました。これらの製品は日本を始め、中国、北米、ヨーロッパの国々で販売されてきました。国別マーケット・シェアは、日本が20パーセント弱、その他の国々では平均5〜10パーセントです。

Notes
- 製品 → 市場 → 市場シェアという流れをつかみたい。
  We have been manufacturing … → Our products are sold in … → Our market share is …
- inception 「創業」
- market share 「市場シェア」

Body 2
企業概要を説明する(続き) → 工場、売上高(伸び率)の説明に使える!

We currently have two domestic production facilities in Chiba and Shizuoka prefectures(国内の工場所在地). We also have overseas plants in China, Mexico and Germany(海外の工場所在地). We supply steering wheels, parts and accessory components(製品) for six major automotive manufacturers(取引先の業種) worldwide. Our total annual sales in 2005(売上高の対象年) surpassed 10 billion(売上高) yen. With our plans for further expansion into the Asian(展開予定の地域) market, particularly in Korea(期待される国名), we expect a 15(売上高増加率)% increase in sales in 2006(対象となる年).

訳　現在、国内には千葉県、静岡県にそれぞれ製造工場があります。さらに海外の工場が中国、メキシコ、ドイツにあります。わが社のハンドル、自動車部品は世界の自動車大手6社に供給されています。2005年の年間売上げは100億円を上回りました。アジア市場での、具体的に申しますと、韓国での新工場の設立により、2006年の売上げも15%増を予想しています。

Notes
- 製品を取引先に供給する場合の公式
  supply 製品 for 取引先 (または to 取引先)
- total annual sales 「年間売上高」
- surpass 「上回る」
- expansion 「拡大」

Conclusion
質問を受け付ける

Allow me to stop here to entertain any questions that you have so far.

訳　それでは、このへんで何かご質問はございますでしょうか。

Notes
- 汎用なのでこのまま覚えて使いたい。
- allow 人 to … 「人に〜することを許可する」。つまりここでは「説明を終えて質問を受け付ける」という意味。
- entertain any questions 「質問を受け付ける」。answer any questionsよりは、しゃれている表現。

TOPIC 16 企業概要Ⅰ——自動車業界

TOPIC 17 企業概要 II
――製薬業界

日本の製薬会社の販売部長である加藤香織さんが、トロントで催された製薬業界の会議で自社の製品について説明をします。

Track 17

Good afternoon. I'm Kaori Kato from Lifestyle Pharmaceuticals, based in Tokyo, Japan. We are a medium-sized pharmaceutical company that manufactures and markets a wide variety of both prescription and over-the-counter dermatological creams and ointments. We are most known in Japan for our non-prescription acne cream ClearSkin.

Our company was formed through a merger of two smaller companies in March 1996. Since then, we have created 14 new products, all of which are still being sold in Japan today. Although we are not currently marketing our products internationally, we are considering breaking into the Canadian market with ClearSkin. These plans are pending approval from the Canadian Ministry of Health.

We have three manufacturing facilities in Japan. Once ClearSkin receives approval in Canada, we will consider the possibility of opening a fourth production plant in Alberta. Assuming that all goes smoothly, this would most likely take place in the spring of 2008.

Please help yourselves to the promotional materials we have here and contact us if you have any questions. Thank you.

解説

Introduction
企業概要を説明する

Good afternoon. I'm Kaori Kato(名前) from Lifestyle Pharmaceuticals(会社名), based in Tokyo, Japan(会社所在地:都市名、国名). We are a medium-sized pharmaceutical company that manufactures and markets a wide variety of both prescription and over-the-counter dermatological creams and ointments(商品名). We are most known in Japan(会社知名度の高い国名) for our non-prescription acne cream ClearSkin(商品名).

訳 皆さん、こんにちは。私は日本の東京にありますライフスタイル製薬の加藤香織と申します。わが社は中堅の製薬会社で、皮膚用クリームと軟膏を、処方箋薬と大衆薬の両方で製造、販売しています。日本では大衆薬として売られているアクネクリーム、「クリアスキン」が最もよく知られています。

Notes
- 自己紹介の変わったパターンも覚えよう！
  名前 from 会社名, based in 会社の所在都市名、国名
  Kaori Kato from Lifestyle Pharmaceuticals, based in Tokyo, Japan
- medium-sized 「中規模の」
- pharmaceutical 「製薬の」
- prescription 「処方箋」
- over-the-counter 「薬局で購入できる」。つまり処方箋なしで買える、ということ。

Body 1
企業設立の経緯、今後のマーケティング方針を説明する

Our company was formed through a merger of two smaller companies in March 1996(合併した年). Since then, we have created 14(開発した製品数) new products, all of which are still being sold in Japan(販売している国) today. Although we are not currently marketing our products internationally, we are considering breaking into the Canadian(進出する国名) market with ClearSkin(商品名). These plans are pending approval from the Canadian Ministry of Health(認可する団体名).

訳 わが社は1996年3月に2つの小さな会社の合併によって生まれました。以来、14の製品を開発し、どれも今日、日本で販売されております。現在海外での販売は行なっておりませんが、「クリアスキン」でカナダ市場への参入を計画中で、カナダ当局に許可証を依頼している最中です。

- be formed through a merger 「合併で生まれる」
- break into … 「～へ参入する」
- 「ペンディングです」に対する英語は、These are pending.「～でペンディングです」と理由をつけるなら、These plans are pending …となる。

Body 2

今後のマーケティング展開について説明する

We have three(工場の数) manufacturing facilities in Japan(工場の所在国). Once ClearSkin(認可を受ける商品名) receives approval in Canada(認可する国名), we will consider the possibility of opening a fourth production plant in Alberta(進出予定地). Assuming that all goes smoothly, this would most likely take place in the spring of 2008(計画が実施される年).

訳 日本国内には3か所の製造工場があります。カナダでの「クリアスキン」の販売許可が下りた暁には、アルバータ州に第4番目の工場を建設する予定です。計画が順調に進めば2008年の春には着工したいと思います。

- receive approval 「許可をもらう」
- consider the possibility of … 「～の可能性を考慮する」
- assuming that all goes smoothly, … 「すべてがうまくいったとして」
- take place 「着工する」

Conclusion

聴衆に資料の入手を促す

Please help yourselves to the promotional materials we have here and contact us if you have any questions. Thank you.

訳 ぜひ、わが社の資料をお手にとってご覧ください。ご質問等、皆さまからのご連絡をお待ち申し上げます。ありがとうございました。

- 汎用的に使えるので、ぜひこのまま覚えたい。
- help yourselves to … 「～をご自由に（おとりください）」
- contact us 「連絡する」

TOPIC 18 企業概要 Ⅲ
——エコツアー会社

エコツアー会社の営業部長が、旅行業界の会議で自社のサービスについて説明します。

Track 18

EcoGlobe provides ecotours to exciting destinations worldwide that offer stunning natural beauty, fascinating wildlife and adventure. Our services are all-inclusive and cover travel, lodging, meals, excursions and more.

We set ourselves apart from the competition by providing custom-designed packages for small groups of six to eight travelers. This tailored service gives our clients the freedom to select the destinations and activities that interest them the most and allows them to fully design their own tours. They can also choose their preferred degree of ruggedness regarding accommodations, ranging from upscale lodges on the edge of the jungle to rustic mountain camping dozens of miles from civilization.

Our mission is to allow our clients to explore the beauty that nature has to offer while simultaneously teaching them how to protect it. We cater to a wide range of customers across multiple market segments. Our total number of clients in 2005 surpassed 9,000. Our client goal for 2006 is to reach 10,000.

Next, I would like to explain each of our services in more detail...

解説

Introduction

サービス内容を説明する

EcoGlobe(会社名) provides ecotours(サービス名) to exciting destinations worldwide that offer stunning natural beauty, fascinating wildlife and adventure(サービス概要). Our services are all-inclusive and cover travel, lodging, meals, excursions and more(サービス内容).

訳 エコグローブ社は世界各地の自然美の素晴らしさ、野生生物や冒険の魅力をお届けするエコツアーを提供しています。わが社のサービスは現地までの往復、宿泊、食事、観光等のすべてが含まれています。

Notes
- provide ＋サービス名 「〜を提供する」
- destinations 「目的地」
- stunning 「素晴らしい」
- all-inclusive 「すべてが含まれる」
- our services cover ＋サービス内容 「サービスは〜を含んでいる」

Body 1

オプション内容を説明する

We set ourselves apart from the competition by providing custom-designed packages for small groups of six to eight(旅行者のグループ人数) travelers. This tailored service gives our clients the freedom to select the destinations and activities(オプション内容) that interest them the most and allows them to fully design their own tours(サービス内容). They can also choose their preferred degree of ruggedness regarding accommodations, ranging from upscale lodges on the edge of the jungle to rustic mountain camping dozens of miles from civilization(特定のオプション内容).

訳 私どものツアーでは6〜8人の小グループの顧客に対してカスタム・デザインしたパッケージを提供している点で、他社とは違ったツアーとなっております。この個別サービスにより顧客は希望の行き先やアクティビティを指定することができ、自分たちに最も合ったツアーを計画することができるわけです。また宿泊施設については顧客の好みにより、ジャングルの端にある高級ホテルから、街から遠く離れた山間でのキャンプなど、さまざまなものの中から選ぶことができます。

Notes
- サービスの極意である「カスタマイズ」の表現は、第1文が参考になる。また、カスタマイズのポイントとなる "the freedom to select" は、第2文に例がある。
- set ourselves apart from … 「〜とは違う」
- tailored 「個別の」
- give our clients the freedom to … 「顧客が自由に〜できる」

Body 2
実績と目標を説明する → 企業ミッションの説明に使える!

Our mission is to allow our clients to explore the beauty that nature has to offer while simultaneously teaching them how to protect it(ミッションの内容). We cater to a wide range of customers across multiple market segments. Our total number of clients in 2005(対象年) surpassed 9,000(顧客数). Our client goal for 2006(対象年) is to reach 10,000(目標顧客数).

訳 わが社が目指しているのは、顧客が自然の美しさにふれるとともに、それをどう守っていくかを学ぶことができるようにすることです。顧客にはいろいろな職業の方がいらっしゃいます。2005年の顧客数は9000人を上回りました。2006年は10,000人を目標にしています。

Notes
- cateringは「仕出し、宅配」の意味だが、cater to … は「〜の要求を満たす、〜に必要なものを供給する」という意味。第1文は、ミッションを説明する定型文。
- mission 「目指すもの、使命」
- simultaneously 「同時に」

Conclusion
追加説明の案内をする

Next, I would like to explain each of our services in more detail...

訳 次に、それぞれのサービスについて、もう少し詳しく説明したいと思います…。

Notes
- スピーチがここで終わらないパターンの表現として覚えておこう。
- in more detail 「さらに詳しく」

TOPIC 19 企業概要 Ⅳ
――化学物質メーカー

化学物質メーカーの副社長が、産業安全に関わる会議で会社の紹介を行ないます。

Track 19

Sunbeam Chemical is a manufacturer of chemical substances used in creating household products such as cleaners, disinfectants, deodorizers and bug repellant. Our corporate philosophy is founded upon two key words: safety and quality.

Since the production of chemicals involves a certain amount of risk, we place employee safety above all else. Over the past 22 years, we have developed stringent procedures for handling chemicals in our refining and production processes. We are proud to say that since our inception we have had no major industrial accidents and we have no intention of letting this change.

As the quality of our chemicals directly impacts the end products purchased by consumers, we also place a high level of importance on quality control. Each of our processes is stringently controlled by thoroughly trained quality control managers to ensure the highest levels of purity in our products.

Allow me to introduce Mr. Jiro Hada, head of our Production Safety Department, to discuss our safety procedures in more detail.

解説

Introduction

企業概要を説明する → 企業哲学の説明に使える!

Sunbeam Chemical(会社名) is a manufacturer of chemical substances used in creating household products such as cleaners, disinfectants, deodorizers and bug repellant(製品と概要). Our corporate philosophy is founded upon two key words: safety and quality(企業理念).

訳 サンビーム・ケミカル社は洗剤、消毒剤、脱臭剤、そして防虫剤などの家庭用品に使われています化学物質を製造しております。わが社の哲学は、安全と品質の2つです。

Notes
- Our corporate philosophy is … 「企業哲学は〜です」
- be founded upon … 「〜のもと、成り立っている」

Body 1

危険物取扱いに関する説明をする → 事故ゼロの実績がある場合に使える!

Since the production of chemicals(製品) involves a certain amount of risk, we place employee safety above all else. Over the past 22 years(開発年数), we have developed stringent procedures for handling chemicals(製品) in our refining and production processes. We are proud to say that since our inception we have had no major industrial accidents and we have no intention of letting this change.

訳 化学物質の製造はいくらかの危険を伴うものですから、何よりも従業員の安全を第一に考えております。過去22年間、精製と製造工程における化学物質の取扱いには非常に厳しい手順を開発してまいりました。お陰さまで創業以来、大きな産業事故もなく、またこれからもそれは受け継いでいくつもりです。

Notes
- 危険物対応の表現
- We place … above all else. 「〜を第一に考える」
- develop stringent procedures 「厳しい手順を開発する」
- We are proud to say that … 何かを誇りに思い、それを称える際の慣用表現。
- inception 「創業」

Body 2

品質管理を説明する

As the quality of our chemicals(製品) directly impacts the end products purchased by consumers, we also place a high level of importance on quality control. Each of our processes is stringently controlled by thoroughly trained quality control managers to ensure the highest levels of purity in our products.

> **訳** わが社の製品の質がそのまま、消費者の手元に届く商品に影響してくるわけですから、品質管理にはとても気をつけています。十分に研修を積んだ品質管理官により各プロセスは厳しく管理されており、製品の質が保たれるように努めています。

Notes
- 品質管理に関する汎用パラグラフとして使える。
- we also place a high level of importance on … 前のパラグラフでも同様の表現がある。類似の内容をいう場合に、表現に幅を持たせたい。

Conclusion

次のスピーカーを紹介する

Allow me to introduce Mr. Jiro Hada(名前), head(肩書き) of our Production Safety Department(部署名), to discuss our safety procedures(話の内容) in more detail.

> **訳** では、製品安全部長の羽田にわが社の安全管理についてもう少し詳しく説明してもらいます。

Notes
- Allow me to … 「〜させてください」という丁寧な表現。
- discussは「話をする」という意味。必ずしもグループで「討議する」ことを指すわけではない。

TOPIC 20 顧客訪問
——サービスの説明

小溝潤さんは、サンフランシスコにある日本の旅行代理店の営業担当で、会社のサービスについて顧客を訪問して説明します。

Track 20

Thank you for asking me to come and speak to you today about the services we offer at Easy Travel. We specialize in full-service travel between Japan and the U.S. and offer some of the lowest fares available.

For your employees traveling both domestically and to Japan for business meetings, we can provide you with hassle-free travel arrangements over the phone and same-day ticketing in most situations. We are also happy to arrange accommodations and rental cars as needed. To give you an idea of the kind of fares we can offer, here is a list of sample fares that we can currently secure for travel within the next month. This includes both travel to Japan as well as to major cities within the U.S.

We have a 24-hour emergency hotline available for our customers for after-hours use in case last-minute changes need to be made at night or on the weekends. Our goal is to provide quality service with maximum flexibility at the lowest price possible.

We have been in business in the Bay Area for over 15 years, and we currently serve the travel needs of over 150 businesses. I'll leave you some basic information that outlines our services as well as my card. Please do not hesitate to call me if we can be of any assistance. Thank you for your time.

解説

Introduction

招いてくれたことに対するお礼、サービス概要

Thank you for asking me to come and speak to you today about the services we offer at Easy Travel(会社名). We specialize in full-service travel between Japan and the U.S.(サービス対象となる国名) and offer some of the lowest fares(サービスのポイント) available.

訳 本日はこちらに伺って、私どもイージー・トラベル社のサービスについてご説明するようにとのご依頼、誠にありがとうございました。私どもは日米間のフルサービスの旅行を専門としています。また最安値の航空券も取り扱っております。

Notes
- services we offer at … 「〜が提供するサービス」。前置詞はatを使う。
- specialize in … 「〜を専門とする」
- fares 「価格」

Body 1

サービス内容の説明

For your employees traveling both domestically and to Japan for business meetings, we can provide you with hassle-free travel(サービスの特徴) arrangements over the phone and same-day ticketing(サービスの特徴) in most situations. We are also happy to arrange accommodations and rental cars(追加サービス内容) as needed. To give you an idea of the kind of fares(サービスの特徴) we can offer, here is a list of sample fares(サービスの特徴) that we can currently secure for travel(サービス) within the next month. This includes both travel to Japan(国名) as well as to major cities within the U.S.(国名)

訳 御社の社員の方々がビジネス・ミーティングでアメリカ国内、および日本へ出張なさる折には、電話一本で、ほとんどの場合、同日発行の航空券を始めとして、ご旅行の手配をさせていただきます。必要に応じて、宿泊先やレンタカーの手配もいたします。ご参考までに、来月中のご出発便に適応できます航空運賃のリストを持ってまいりました。日本行きの便とアメリカ国内の主な都市への便の運賃です。

Notes
- このパラグラフは、旅行業界に特化したものだが、一般的なサービスの中でも、特に価格に関する説明は汎用的に使える。
- provide you with … arrangements over the phone 「〜は電話で対応可」

- hassle-free 「手間のかからない」
- same-day … 「同日中に〜できる」
- arrange … as needed 「必要に応じて〜対応可」
- here is a list of sample … 「〜のサンプルのリストがあります」

Body 2
電話サービスの説明

We have a 24-hour emergency hotline available for our customers for after-hours use in case last-minute changes need to be made at night or on the weekends. Our goal is to provide quality service with maximum flexibility at the lowest price possible.

> **訳** わが社にはお客さま向け24時間緊急直通電話があります。夜中や週末など営業時間外に、急なご旅行の変更をなさりたいときに使っていただけます。私どもはできるだけ低価格で最大の柔軟性を持った質の高いサービスを心がけております。

> **Notes**
> - 24時間電話サービスについての説明は、このパラグラフで十分事足りる。
> - after-hours 「営業時間外」を指す。
> - last-minute changes 「最後の1分」。つまり「直前の変更」という意味。ちなみに、last-minute cancellationはいわゆる「ドタキャン」のこと。
> - maximum flexibility 「最大の柔軟性」

Conclusion
会社概要と今後の対応

We have been in business in the Bay Area (営業している地域) for over 15 (営業年数) years, and we currently serve the travel (サービス) needs of over 150 (顧客企業数) businesses. I'll leave you some basic information that outlines our services as well as my card. Please do not hesitate to call me if we can be of any assistance. Thank you for your time.

> **訳** ベイ・エリアで15年以上、現在150社を超えるお客様とお取引させていただいております。わが社のサービスを説明した簡単なパンフレットと私の名刺を置いてまいりますので、何かございましたら、ぜひご連絡ください。よろしくお願いいたします。

TOPIC 20 顧客訪問──サービスの説明

Notes
- be in business in … for 〜 years 「〜年にわたり、…で（通常は「地域」が入る）ビジネスをしている」
- serve … needs of over 〜 businesses 「〜社以上の、…のニーズに応える」
- outline … 「〜の概略を説明する」
- my card 「名刺」
- if we can be of any assistance 「何かございましたら」。構文の点では、一風変わった表現。

TOPIC 21 説得 I
―― セールストーク

コピー機の営業マンが大阪の小さな英国資本企業に対し、もっといいコピー機を使うようにセールストークを行なっています。

Track 21

I see that you are currently using our XR-2000. This is a good copier, but you may want to consider upgrading to a model with higher performance given the growth that your company has been achieving.

Let me show you some of the products in our EZ-Speed line of copiers. All of these models function as a copier, color printer and fax. Since you often print and copy rather lengthy documents, I would strongly recommend the EZ-Speed III. It prints at a rate of 30 pages per minute. The cost runs a bit more than the machine you have now, but given your demand for speedy printing and copying, it would pay for itself by saving you time in the long run. I think that it is definitely worth considering.

If you would prefer something that is more space efficient, we also have the EZ-Speed Petit. Its output speed doesn't quite match up to the EZ-Speed III, but it takes up a lot less space. This is another option you might want to think about.

Why don't I leave you this brochure and let you think things over? In the meantime, don't hesitate to call me if you have any questions.

解説

Introduction
製品の紹介

I see that you are currently using our XR-2000(製品モデル). This is a good copier(製品名), but you may want to consider upgrading to a model with higher performance given the growth that your company has been achieving.

> **訳** 現在、わが社のXR-2000をお使いいただいているようですね。この機種もいいものですが、成長を遂げている御社にぴったりの、さらにアップグレードしたモデルに買い換えることをお考えになってはいかがでしょう。

> **Notes**
> - コピー機の例となっているが、コピー機以外にも使えるスピーチである。使用機器のアップグレード（upgrading）を提案している。ちなみに、「グレードアップ」は和製英語。
> - you may want to … 助言、提言などを表わす丁寧な言い方。
> - upgrade to … 「～にアップグレードする」
> - given … 条件、前提について言う場合に使える。

Body 1
提案する製品の機能説明

Let me show you some of the products in our EZ-Speed(製品シリーズ名) line of copiers. All of these models function as a copier, color printer and fax(具体的な機能名). Since you often print and copy rather lengthy documents, I would strongly recommend the EZ-Speed III. It prints at a rate of 30 pages per minute. / The cost runs a bit more than the machine you have now, but given your demand for speedy printing and copying(機能), it would pay for itself by saving you time in the long run. I think that it is definitely worth considering.

> **訳** ここで、わが社の「EZスピード」シリーズのコピー機をいくつかご紹介させていただきます。すべてのモデルにコピー機、カラープリンター、そしてファックス機能を持たせました。皆さまは普段、かなりの枚数の書類のプリントやコピーをなさっているようなので、ぜひ、「EZスピードⅢ」を使ってみてください。これですと、1分間に30枚のプリントが可能です。今お使いの機種よりも若干経費が掛かりますが、プリントとコピーの時間短縮により、長い目で見れば経費削減に役立つと思います。どうか、ご一考ください。

Notes
- スラッシュ（／）以降は汎用ケースで、そのまま使える例となっている。I think that it is definitely worth considering. はよく使われるセールストークのひとつ。
- function as …　「～として機能する」
- lengthy documents　「かなりの枚数の書類」
- at a rate of … per minute　「1分間に～の」
- the cost runs a bit more　「経費が若干掛かる」
- pay for itself　「経費削減する」「元がとれる」
- worth considering　「一考に値する」

Body 2
別製品の提案

If you would prefer something that is more space efficient, we also have the EZ-Speed Petit(別製品名). Its output speed doesn't quite match up to the EZ-Speed III, but it takes up a lot less space. This is another option you might want to think about.

訳　もし、もう少し小型の機種がご希望でしたら、「EZスピード・プティ」はいかがでしょうか。プリントのスピードは「EZスピードⅢ」に比べると劣りますが、置き場所をかなり節約することができます。こちらも選択肢に加えていただければと思います。

Notes
- space efficient　「空間的に効率的な」。つまり「小型の」という意味。
- output　「出力」。ここでは「プリント」。
- take up a lot less space　「少ない空間をとる」。つまり「置き場所を節約できる」。
- 最後の文章はセールストークのまとめにふさわしい。ここでは、might want to … が使われている。

Conclusion
資料の提示と質問をうながす

Why don't I leave you this brochure and let you think things over? In the meantime, don't hesitate to call me if you have any questions.

訳　この商品カタログを置いてまいりますので、よろしければどうぞご検討ください。その間、ご質問等ございましたら、私までお電話ください。

Notes
- 参考資料を置いて検討材料にするケースで使える、まとめのパラグラフ。
- leave you this brochure　「カタログを置いておく」

TOPIC 21　説得Ⅰ──セールストーク

TOPIC 22 説得 II ―人事

東京にある米国資本の投資銀行地域部長が、上海への転勤が伴う昇進を受けるように、ある従業員を説得しようとしています。

Track 22

Now Mike, I know your initial reaction to this opportunity was negative, but I'd like you to please give it some more consideration. I think that if you look at it carefully, you'll clearly see that the pros outweigh the cons.

I understand that you and your family have finally just become settled here in Tokyo. But, even if you pass up this position in Shanghai, you know that you'll probably return to New York in two or three years anyway. Your kids are still very young, so I'm sure they would have no problem with the adjustment.

Think of what you'd be gaining out of this. You would get a 15% increase in salary, we could offer you a much more spacious apartment in Shanghai, and you would also be given a company car for your own personal use.

Yes, I know that the new position will require you to spend more hours at the office, but think of all the fantastic venture capital experience you'll be getting in China, Mike. I really don't think you should pass this up. Sleep on it and we can talk more about it tomorrow.

解説

Introduction

説得を試みる

Now Mike(相手の名前), I know your initial reaction to this opportunity was negative, but I'd like you to please give it some more consideration. I think that if you look at it carefully, you'll clearly see that the pros outweigh the cons.

訳 さてマイク、この話にはあまり乗り気じゃなかったようだが、もう少し考えてみてもらえないだろうか。よく考えると、これは君にとって損なことより、得なことの方が多いはずなんだけどな。

Notes
- 相手の反応を読み取って（reaction → negative）、それに対して説得し始める。拒否反応を起こすのではなく、よく検討し（give it some more consideration）、そのためには注意深く見て（look at it carefully）、いかにprosがconsを上回るかを自ら認識させる必要がある。
- "pros and cons"（賛否）は、内容を比較検討する際によく用いられる手法で、いわゆるディベート的な発想。Advantages and disadvantages, good points and bad pointsという白黒の違いをよく理解し比較することで、客観的に見てどちらが自分にとって有利な条件かを見きわめるやり方。
- outweigh … 「〜に優る」

Body 1

家族をダシに説得する

I understand that you and your family have finally just become settled here in Tokyo(所在地). But, even if you pass up this position in Shanghai(駐在地), you know that you'll probably return to New York(都市名) in two or three(駐在年数) years anyway. Your kids are still very young, so I'm sure they would have no problem with the adjustment.

訳 ご家族も皆さんやっと東京に慣れて落ち着いたことは承知しているよ。ただ、この上海のポジションを辞退してもどのみち、おそらく2、3年後にはニューヨークに戻ることはわかっているよね。君の子供たちもまだ小さいんだし、新しい生活に慣れるのになんの心配もないと思うんだがね。

Notes
- become settled 「落ち着く」
- pass up … 「〜を辞退する」
- adjustment 「適応すること」「慣れること」

TOPIC 22

説得II ── 人事

TOPIC 22 説得Ⅱ——人事

Body 2
条件から説得する

Think of what you'd be gaining out of this. You would get a 15(昇給率)% increase in salary, we could offer you a much more spacious apartment in Shanghai(駐在地), and you would also be given a company car for your own personal use.

> **訳** この昇進で得るものを考えてみたまえ。給料は15％上がる。上海ではもっと広い部屋に住める。それに、社用車を自家用車として使えることにもなるんだよ。

Notes
- gain out of … 「～から得る」
- 昇給（get a 15% increase in salary）
  → 広い住まい（spacious apartment）→ 社用車（a company car）
- for your own personal use 「自家用」

Conclusion
説得を続ける

Yes, I know that the new position will require you to spend more hours at the office, but think of all the fantastic venture capital experience you'll be getting in China(駐在国), Mike(相手の名前). I really don't think you should pass this up. Sleep on it and we can talk more about it tomorrow.

> **訳** もちろん、会社にいる時間が増えるのは確かだ。でも、中国でベンチャーキャピタルの経験ができるなんて、こんな素晴らしいことはないじゃないか、マイク。これは辞退すべきではないな。ひと晩よく考えて、明日また話し合おう。

Notes
- 前のパラグラフで具体的な数字を示した後は、そのまとめとしてさらに説得を続けている。プラスの面ばかりではない。労働時間が長くなる（spend more hours at the office）というマイナス面も予想される。即答を求めているのではない。ゆっくり考え（sleep on it）、また話し合いは続く（talk more about it tomorrow）。

> **POINT**
>
> ## 家族とビジネス
>
> 一般的な英語圏の発想として、家族はビジネス同様、大切です。その逆手をとって、家族をダシに説得する方法もあります。スモールトークでは、家族について聞かれることがあるので、恥ずかしいなどと思わず、話せるようにしておきましょう。日本通の相手だったら理解を示してくれるでしょうが、自分や自分の家族のことを「卑下する」のを奇異に思う場合がありますので、それは慎むようにしましょう。

TOPIC 22 説得Ⅱ──人事

TOPIC 23 新営業所開設
――発表

（株）昭和トレーディングはシアトルに新しい営業所を開設することになり、米国西海岸地域統括本部長の近藤浩志氏が、ロサンゼルス営業所の従業員を集めて報告をします。

Track 23

Good morning. As manager for the West Coast region of Showa Trading, I am pleased to announce plans to open a new office in Seattle in the latter part of this year.

Our business has been booming in the Pacific Rim over the past two years. As a result, our Los Angeles office alone cannot handle the volume of imports arriving at our West Coast ports from Asia. To alleviate this problem, we have decided to open a new distribution center in Seattle.

This office will coordinate all goods that arrive in Seattle. I know that many of you have been overworked during the past year since you have been overseeing logistics for both Los Angeles and Seattle. The creation of the new office should take much of this weight off your shoulders.

We will have about 20 positions to fill to staff the new office. We will consider in-house candidates first, so I encourage anybody who is interested to apply. The positions will be announced next month. Thank you for your attention.

解説

Introduction

発表する

Good morning. As manager for the West Coast region of Showa Trading(会社名), I am pleased to announce plans to open a new office in Seattle(支店所在地) in the latter part of this year(開設時期).

訳 皆さん、おはようございます。昭和トレーディング西海岸地域統括本部長として、今年度後期にシアトルの営業所を開設することをここに発表いたします。

Notes
- I'm pleased to announce … 発表の定型表現として覚えておきたい。
- open a new office 「営業所の新規開設」。場所も開設時期も前置詞inで表現する。
- in the latter part of … 「〜の後期に」

Body 1

好況の背景や状況を説明する

Our business has been booming in the Pacific Rim(地域名) over the past two years(期間). As a result, our Los Angeles(支店名) office alone cannot handle the volume of imports arriving at our West Coast ports(納品される場所) from Asia. To alleviate this problem, we have decided to open a new distribution center in Seattle(所在地).

訳 わが社はここ2年ほど環太平洋においてシェアを広げてまいりました。その結果、ロサンゼルス営業所だけでは、アジアから西海岸の港に運ばれてくる輸入品を処理することができなくなりました。この問題を緩和するためにシアトルに流通センターを開設することになった次第です。

Notes
- boom 「シェアを広げる」
- handle the volume "ボリューム"は音量ではなく、「数量」を指す。
- alleviate this problem 「問題を緩和させる」
- このパラグラフから、次の論理展開が読み取れただろうか。
  原因 → 結果（問題）→ 対策

Body 2
開設する営業所の役割を説明する

This office will coordinate all goods that arrive in Seattle (納品される場所). I know that many of you have been overworked during the past year since you have been overseeing logistics for both Los Angeles and Seattle (都市名). The creation of the new office should take much of this weight off your shoulders.

> **訳** 当営業所ではシアトルに運搬される商品をすべて取り扱うことになります。ここにいらっしゃる多くの皆さんがロサンゼルスとシアトル両地区の業務をこなすために、この1年過重労働をされていたことを認識しております。この新営業所の開設により、かなり仕事の量が減らされることでしょう。

> **Notes**
> - You have been overworked … 「働きすぎだった」
> - logistics 「物流管理」
> - take much of this weight off your shoulders 「肩から重荷を取り除く」が本来の意味。

Conclusion
募集を行なう

We will have about 20 (募集人数) positions to fill to staff the new office. We will consider in-house candidates first, so I encourage anybody who is interested to apply. The positions will be announced next month (募集開始時期). Thank you for your attention.

> **訳** 新営業所の職員は約20名を予定しています。現在わが社で働いていらっしゃる皆さんをまず、候補者として募りますので、どうか興味のある方は応募してください。新しい職種については来月発表いたします。よろしくお願いします。

> **Notes**
> - fillするpositionがある、という発想がおもしろい。
> - in-house (社内の) に対することばとしてfreelance (フリーランス) がある。

> **POINT**
>
> ## PDCAを回す
>
> このスピーチは、問題解決型の思考回路をうまく使って作られています。
>
> 　現状分析 → 原因特定 → 対策検討 → 問題解決
>
> ビジネスの世界では、「PDCAを回す」とよく言われますが、それに相当するでしょう。ちなみに、PDCAのPはPlan（計画）、DはDo（実行）、CはCheck（評価）、AはAction（対策）のアクロニム（頭字語）です。

TOPIC 23 新営業所開設――発表

TOPIC 24 工場閉鎖
──発表

自動車部品メーカーの米国製造本部長の藤田正太郎さんが工場で働く職員に対して、ケンタッキーの工場を閉鎖することを発表します。

Track 24

Good afternoon. My name is Shotaro Fujita, head of manufacturing operations in the U.S. Last year marked the 15th anniversary of the establishment of this facility here in Kentucky. Almost half of you have been with us since our first day of operations, and I commend you for your dedication over the years.

The fact that many of you have been here for so long makes what I have to say all the more difficult. Due to rising costs in maintaining this production facility and a steady decrease in sales over the past two years, we have made the decision to close this plant by the end of the year.

We have tried everything financially possible to avoid having to close the plant, but in the end this is our only option. Making a decision that results in putting excellent employees out of work is always a difficult one to have to make.

We are putting together details regarding the severance packages that we will be able to offer. We will try to be as generous as possible given all that you have done for us over the years.

I thank you for your hard work and loyalty.

解説

Introduction

自己紹介、工場の歴史を説明する

Good afternoon. My name is Shotaro Fujita(名前), head(役職) of manufacturing operations in the U.S.(業務名、所在地) Last year(設立年数を数えた年) marked the 15th(設立年数) anniversary of the establishment of this facility here in Kentucky(工場の設立地). Almost half(設立以来の勤務者数) of you have been with us since our first day of operations, and I commend you for your dedication over the years.

訳　こんにちは。米国製造本部長を務めます藤田正太郎と申します。昨年、このケンタッキー工場は設立15周年を迎えました。ここにいらっしゃる半分に近い従業員の方々が工場設立当初から働いてくださっています。皆さんが今までわが社のために働いてくださったことは本当にありがたいことと感謝いたしております。

Notes
- mark 「しるしをつける」。Mark your calendar.（カレンダーにしるしをつけなさい）。予定を忘れないようにカレンダーに書き込んでおくよう依頼する表現。
- have been with us　ここでは「従業員として働いている」という意味。講義、授業などで、相手がしっかり聞いているかどうかを確認する表現に"Are you with me?"がある。簡単な表現だが、多用されるので、ぜひ覚えておこう。
- I commend you for your dedication over the years.　貢献を称える定型文として覚えておこう。

Body 1

工場閉鎖に至る理由を説明する

The fact that many of you have been here for so long makes what I have to say all the more difficult. Due to rising costs in maintaining this production facility(経費対象) and a steady decrease in sales(減少がみられる分野) over the past two(減少がみられる年数) years, we have made the decision to close this plant by the end of the year(閉鎖する時期).

訳　多くの皆さんがこれだけ長く我々と一緒に働いてこられたことを思うと、これから申し上げなければならないことがなお一層お伝えしにくくなります。年々増えていく当工場の経費とこの2年の減り続ける売上げを鑑み、今年末までに当工場は閉鎖することになりました。

Notes
- [Introduction] で長年にわたる就労をねぎらい、それを受けて、[Body 1] では、「長らく働いてもらっているから、これから発表することが残念だ」と続けている。このようなスムーズな論理展開は実際なかなか表現するのがむずかしいので、サンプルを真似ることから始めたい。
- rising costs 「増える経費」
- steady 「一定の」。つまりここでは「減る一方の」という意味。
- close 「閉鎖する」

Body 2
以下が唯一の解決策であることを説明する

We have tried everything financially possible to avoid having to close the plant, but in the end this is our only option. Making a decision that results in putting excellent employees out of work is always a difficult one to have to make.

訳 我々は工場閉鎖を免れるべく、できる限りの資金調達を試みてまいりましたが、最終的にこのような結果を強いられることとなりました。皆さんのように優秀な従業員の方々に辞めていただく決断を下すのは本当に心苦しいことです。

Notes
- try everything 「すべて試みる」
- This is our only option 「唯一の手段である」
- put 人 out of work 「職を失わせる」（=lose *one's* job)
- 工場閉鎖に対して予想される抗議を想定し、できるだけ従業員のことを思いやった内容にする。
- 最善を尽くした → 唯一の対策である → 対策が失業者を生む → 心苦しい

Conclusion
今後の対策について説明する

We are putting together details regarding the severance packages（解職対応の内容） that we will be able to offer. We will try to be as generous as possible given all that you have done for us over the years.
I thank you for your hard work and loyalty.

訳 会社の方から提供できる解職に関するさまざまな件につきましては、これから細かい点を詰めていきます。長年、わが社のために尽くしてこられた皆さんに、できるだけのことをさせていただきたいと思っています。
これまでのお勤め、本当にご苦労さまでした。

Notes
- put together 「まとめる」「検討する」
- generous ということばは、「気前のよい」「寛大な」の意味。「太っ腹」にも相当する。
- given all that … 「〜という条件をもってすれば」。given は「（何かを）与えた」という過去分詞ではなく、provided that …, with … と同様に、「〜を条件として」という条件節を構成する表現。

TOPIC 24

工場閉鎖——発表

TOPIC 25 支店開設
——お知らせ

次のスピーチは新しい支店開設のお知らせについてです。

Track 25

Good afternoon. As all of you here in the Marketing Department know, we have been expanding our presence in Southeast Asia over the past few years. I am proud to announce that as part of our latest expansion we will be opening a new office in Singapore in February of next year.

Although the office will eventually be staffed primarily by local employees once it is up and running, we will be sending about 20 staff members from our Tokyo office during the first year to get things off the ground.

In deciding who will be selected to open the Singapore office, we will first consider volunteers for these positions. Within the next week, we will be circulating a memo with detailed job descriptions of all positions available. Please have a look and contact HR if you are interested in applying for any of these openings.

Let me add that we will of course cover all of your moving expenses both to Singapore and back to Japan. We will provide you with a generous monthly housing allowance, in addition to a monthly stipend for living expenses. We encourage both non-Japanese and Japanese employees here at the Tokyo office to apply.

After receiving the memo, please feel free to contact me directly if you have any questions regarding the positions. Thank you.

解説

Introduction

支店開設の発表をする

Good afternoon. As all of you here in the Marketing Department(部署名) know, we have been expanding our presence in Southeast Asia(ターゲット市場) over the past few years(発展期間). I am proud to announce that as part of our latest expansion we will be opening a new office in Singapore(所在地) in February of next year(開設時期).

訳 こんにちは。ここにいらっしゃるマーケティング部の方々のご存知のとおり、わが社はこの数年で東南アジアでのシェアを伸ばしてまいりました。このシェア拡大の最新の動きといたしまして、来年2月にシンガポール支店を立ち上げますことをここに発表いたします。

Notes
- expand our presence in … 「〜でのシェアを伸ばす」
- I am proud to announce that … 発表のキーフレーズ。英語では pride, be proud to … は業績を称える際に多用される。
- open a new office 「新規支店を開設する」

Body 1

当初の計画の説明をする

Although the office will eventually be staffed primarily by local employees once it is up and running, we will be sending about 20(送るスタッフの人数) staff members from our Tokyo(スタッフの所属地) office during the first year to get things off the ground.

訳 一度立ち上がればシンガポール支店の運営は最終的にはそのほとんどを現地採用の従業員に任せていきますが、運営が軌道に乗るまでのはじめの1年間は東京支店から約20名のスタッフを送ることになります。

Notes
- eventually 「最終的には」
- be up and running 「機能して、稼働して」。響きがいいため、このようなセットで、特に口語では使われる。
- get things off the ground 「軌道に乗る」。他に、fly（プロジェクトがうまくいく）という動詞がある。説明している状況としては、同じようなものだろう。

Body 2
希望者を募る

In deciding who will be selected to open the Singapore(支店名) office, we will first consider volunteers for these positions. Within the next week(期間), we will be circulating a memo with detailed job descriptions of all positions available. Please have a look and contact HR if you are interested in applying for any of these openings.

訳 シンガポール支社開設に携わるスタッフの選考方法ですが、まず皆さんの中から希望者を募ろうと思います。来週いっぱい、新しい職種についての細かい仕事内容の説明書を回覧いたしますので、興味のある職種がありましたら、人事部へご連絡ください。

Notes
- volunteers 日本語の「ボランティア」とはちょっと意味が違う。英語では、「希望者」「志願者」に近い。動詞にしてWho wants to volunteer?と言えば「どなたかやりたい方はいますか」となる。
- circulate a memo 「説明書を回覧する」
- detailed job descriptions 「仕事内容を書いたもの」。日本の商習慣にはない考え方。あったとしても、仕事内容は実際、あいまいなものとなるのが一般的な傾向である。
- of all positions available 「新しいすべての職種」。名詞＋availableは、よく使われる形。
- HR=Human Resources 「人事部」。
  HRMはHuman Resources Managementの略で「人事管理」。
- apply for … 「～に応募する」

Body 3
手当を説明する、応募を募る

Let me add that we will of course cover all of your moving expenses both to Singapore and back to Japan(支払われる費用). We will provide you with a generous monthly housing allowance(手当), in addition to a monthly stipend for living expenses. We encourage both non-Japanese and Japanese employees here at the Tokyo(支社名) office to apply.

訳 シンガポール・東京間の往復の引越し費用はもちろん、月給の他に、相当額の住宅手当も支払われることになります。東京支社から日本人、また日本人でない社員の皆さんにもご応募いただきたく、お願い申し上げます。

Notes
- Let me add that … 「それに加えて、〜」。In addition to …, Plus, …, On top of that, … などの表現も覚えよう。
- cover … 「〜が支給の対象となる」という意味。
- moving expenses 「引越し費用」。costを「費用」、expenseを「経費」と勘定科目上分けて考える方法もあるが、本書では特に区別しない。
- housing allowance 「住宅手当」。allowanceは「おこづかい」の意味。
- monthly stipend 「月給」

Conclusion
質問を促す

After receiving the memo, please feel free to contact me directly if you have any questions regarding the positions. Thank you.

訳 回覧される業務内容の説明書について、何かご質問がありましたら、私の方まで直接ご連絡ください。ありがとうございました。

Notes
- please feel free to … = do not hesitate to … 「遠慮なく〜してください」

> **POINT**
> ### やるのは私の仕事だけ
> 日本以外では、「住宅手当」は耳慣れないはず。国民全員加入の保険制度がない国も多いので、企業での保険加入はとてもうれしい条件となります。お茶汲みは女性の仕事だとすれば、今では問題となりますが、昔の日本社会では当然の考え方でした。その発想を海外に持ち込んでしまったある駐在員が、"That is not in my job description." と言われ、お茶汲みを断わられました。その対処法として、「どうしたら、お茶をいれてくれるのか？」と逆にたずねると、「お茶汲み」を "job description" の中に入れてほしいと言われた、というエピソードがあります。"job description" の中の作業は責任を持ってやるが、それ以外の作業はやらない、という発想がなんともおもしろいですね。

TOPIC 25 支店開設——お知らせ

TOPIC 26 日本からの代表団が海外の企業へ行く

日本のパソコンメーカーの代表団が、中国のボタンとスイッチの供給先を訪問します。団を代表して、団長がひと言挨拶をします。

Track 26

Good morning, President Lin, Vice-President Jang and other distinguished executives and directors of Lin Computer Switches Corporation. On behalf of our delegation, I would like to thank you for taking the time to meet with us in person and give us a tour of your facilities. We are pleased to finally meet you face to face after so many months of correspondence via e-mail and telephone.

As you know, we are gradually achieving a greater presence in the Chinese personal computer market. Our new production facility in Shanghai will open next year, so we are now looking for outstanding companies to partner with us as suppliers. After conducting a detailed review of your company during the past several months, we feel that you certainly demonstrate the know-how and reliability that we are looking for.

Allow me to introduce Kenji Yamada, Director of Production. He will be in charge of evaluating your production facilities and making a final recommendation to the Board of Directors upon our return to Japan.

Again, thank you for your time and gracious hospitality. We look forward to a productive visit that will hopefully lead to a fruitful partnership between our two companies.

解説

Introduction
訪問に対する感謝

Good morning, President Lin(社長の名前), Vice-President Jang(副社長の名前) and other distinguished executives and directors of Lin Computer Switches Corporation(会社名). On behalf of our delegation, I would like to thank you for taking the time to meet with us in person and give us a tour of your facilities. We are pleased to finally meet you face to face after so many months of correspondence via e-mail and telephone.

訳 リン社長、ジャン副社長、それからリン・コンピュータ・スイッチズ・コーポレーションの役員の皆さん、おはようございます。団を代表いたしまして、このたび、お時間をとってこうしてお会いくださること、また御社の施設を見学させていただくことに感謝の意を表します。数か月におよぶEメールや電話でのやりとりの後、こうしてじかにお会いすることができますことをうれしく思っています。

Notes
- distinguished 「高貴な」
- on behalf of … 「～を代表して」。組織の代表としてスピーチする場合の決まり文句なので覚えておこう。
- delegation 「団」
- take the time to meet with us 「面会する時間をさく」。日本語でも同様の表現をするので、そのまま覚えておける。
- in person 「顔をつき合わせて」
- correspondence via e-mail and telephone 「Eメールと電話でのやりとり」

Body 1
会社紹介

As you know, we are gradually achieving a greater presence in the Chinese personal computer(業種名) market. Our new production facility in Shanghai(都市名) will open next year(工場開設時期), so we are now looking for outstanding companies to partner with us as suppliers. After conducting a detailed review of your company during the past several months(調査実施期間), we feel that you certainly demonstrate the know-how and reliability that we are looking for.

訳 すでにご存知のことと思いますが、わが社の中国におけるパソコン市場のシェアは徐々に伸びてきています。来年には上海の新しい工場が始動します。そこで部品の供給先としてわが社と組んでくださる優良企業を探して

います。数か月間、御社についていろいろ検討させていただきましたが、技術知識や信頼度において御社は真に私たちが望んでいる会社です。

Notes
- achieve a greater presence in … 「～におけるプレゼンスを達成する」。つまり「シェアを拡大する」という意味。
- outstanding 「優良な」。会計では「未払いの」という意味で使われる。
- conduct a detailed review of … 「～について詳細に検討する」
- demonstrate 「持ち合わせている」
- ITシステムの要件には次のようなものが挙げられる。

• Reliability	「信頼性」
• Availability	「使用可能度、可用性」
• Scalability	「拡張性」
• Portability	「可搬性、携帯性」

Body 2
関係者の紹介

Allow me to introduce Kenji Yamada(名前), Director of Production(役職、部署名). He will be in charge of evaluating your production facilities and making a final recommendation to the Board of Directors upon our return to Japan(国名).

訳 こちらは山田健二と申しまして、わが社の製造部長を務めております。御社の生産工場についての評価を担当し、日本に帰って取締役会に最終報告を行ないます。

Notes
- allow me to … 「～させてください」
- be in charge of … 「～を担当する」
- evaluate 「評価する」
- make a final recommendation to … 「～に最終報告する」
- upon *one's* return to … 「～に帰ってから」

Conclusion
締めのことば

Again, thank you for your time and gracious hospitality. We look forward to a productive visit that will hopefully lead to a fruitful partnership between our two companies.

訳 最後にもう一度、時間をさいてくださったこと、そして皆さんの心のこもったおもてなしに感謝いたします。この訪問が実り多きものとなりますこと、そして願わくば我々2社が良きパートナーとなれますことを期待しています。

Notes
- 企業提携に関してのまとめのことばにふさわしいので、そのまま覚えておきたい。
- hospitality 「おもてなし」
- fruitful 「実り多き」

TOPIC 27 日本からの代表団への歓迎スピーチ

日本のパソコンメーカーの代表団が、中国のボタンとスイッチの供給会社を訪問しています。中国側の会社の社長が日本側団長からの挨拶を受けて、歓迎のスピーチをします。

Track 27

Thank you, President Nomura, for your kind words. I would like to welcome all of you to China. We have been looking forward to your visit for several weeks now and are pleased to finally meet you face to face.

We are very excited by the prospect of becoming your main supplier of computer switches and keyboard buttons. Your reputation as a personal computer manufacturer is very widespread in China and it would be an honor to work with you.

We have planned a few presentations this morning by our Manufacturing Department to provide you with a better understanding of our production process. After answering any questions you have about the presentations, we will go to lunch and then spend most of the afternoon touring the production floor so that you can observe our processes first hand. We will then return here to the conference room and entertain any questions you have about what you see during the tour.

Again, it is a pleasure and an honor to have you with us today. I hope that your visit will be a very positive experience that will help foster a long-lasting partnership between us.

解説

Introduction

歓迎のことば

Thank you, President Nomura(役職、名前), for your kind words. I would like to welcome all of you to China(国名). We have been looking forward to your visit for several weeks(訪問の期間) now and are pleased to finally meet you face to face.

> 訳　野村社長、心のこもったおことばをありがとうございました。皆さん、中国へようこそいらっしゃいました。何週間も前から皆さんのご訪問を社員一同心待ちにしておりましたので、こうしてようやくお会いできて、光栄でございます。

> Notes
> - look forward to your visit 「訪問を楽しみにする」。通常は、挨拶やメールの最後に用いられる表現だが、ここでは、「ずっと楽しみにしてきた」という意味で現在完了進行形（have been looking forward to …）が使われている。
> - finally meet you face to face 「ようやく、じかに会う」。face to faceは、電話やEメールではなく、顔と顔を直接つき合わせて、という意味。

Body 1

協業できることへの期待

We are very excited by the prospect of becoming your main supplier of computer switches and keyboard buttons(製品名). Your reputation as a personal computer manufacturer(業種) is very widespread in China(国名) and it would be an honor to work with you.

> 訳　御社のコンピュータのスイッチとキーボード・ボタンを供給させていただくことになるかもしれない、ということを私たちはとてもうれしく思っています。御社のパソコンメーカーとしての評判は中国内に広まっていますし、ご一緒に仕事をさせていただけましたなら本当に光栄でございます。

> Notes
> - be excited by …　ビジネスでも十分使える表現。be thrilled to … ともいう。
> - prospect 「見通し」
> - reputation 「評判」
> - it would be an honor to …　「〜できて光栄です」

TOPIC 27　日本からの代表団への歓迎スピーチ

Body 2
予定の説明

We have planned a few presentations this morning by our Manufacturing（部署名） Department to provide you with a better understanding of our production process. After answering any questions you have about the presentations, we will go to lunch and then spend most of the afternoon touring the production floor so that you can observe our processes first hand. We will then return here to the conference room and entertain any questions you have about what you see during the tour.

> **訳** 今日は午前中に製造部門よりいくつかのご報告がございますので、わが社の製造工程をよりよくご理解いただけたらと思います。皆さんからのご質問にお答えしたあと、昼食をとります。午後はほとんどを生産工場での実際の生産工程見学に費やしていただきます。その後、再びこの会議室に戻って工場見学で気が付かれた点について、ご質問があれば、それにお答えしたいと思います。

> **Notes**
> - よくある予定についての説明なので、細かな表現は別として、全体の流れは自分で説明できるようになりたい。
>   プレゼンによる生産工程の説明 → プレゼンに関する質問 → 昼食 → 工場見学 → 見学に関しての質問
> - provide 人 with 物　「人に物を提供する」
> - go to lunch　「昼食をとる」
> - tour　「見学をする」
> - observe … first hand　「実際に〜を見る」
> - entertain any questions　「質問を受け付ける」

Conclusion
感謝と結びのことば

Again, it is a pleasure and an honor to have you with us today. I hope that your visit will be a very positive experience that will help foster a long-lasting partnership between us.

> **訳** 今日、皆さんをお迎えできたことはわが社にとって、とても光栄なことであります。どうか今回のご訪問が良い結果を生みますよう、そして御社とこれからも長いお付き合いをさせていただけるよう願っております。

> **Notes**
> - 感謝の意を述べる定型表現: Thank you for …, It is a pleasure to …, It is an honor to …
> - positive experience 「良い経験」「良い結果」
> - foster a long-lasting partnership 「長く続くパートナーシップを培っていく」

⋛POINT

short-termか、long-termか

日本式経営はlong-term perspective、欧米式経営はshort-term perspectiveと対照視されます。はたして、それは正しいのでしょうか。日本経済の繁栄を材料に長期的な視点が尊ばれてきましたが、最近の日本経済の失墜を踏まえて考えると、長期的な視点が必ずしも正しいとはいえません。アジア諸国が他の歴史の浅い地域と比べ、長期的な付き合いを重んじるのは、おそらく、その長い歴史によるところが大きいのでしょう。

TOPIC 27　日本からの代表団への歓迎スピーチ

TOPIC 28 プロジェクト開始
――ミーティングでの挨拶

大手自動車会社の広報部長が新しい広告キャンペーンについてオーストラリア、北米、英国各地域の広報部長と日本でミーティングを行ないます。

Track 28

Good morning, ladies and gentlemen. First of all, thank you all for making the effort to attend this meeting to discuss the start of our new advertising campaign "Drive on the edge!" We will launch this campaign exactly one month from today using TV, radio and print media. This will be a full-scale, global campaign, targeting all English-speaking countries where our cars are sold. The target segment will be primarily single males and females from 25 to 35 who are looking to add some spice to their lives with a stylish, sporty automobile.

The TV commercial that will be used initially is currently in production and will be ready for the campaign launch date next month. It depicts a young female in her late 20s driving along a coastal highway with three friends in the car. They arrive at a beach, unload scuba equipment from the back, gear up and plunge into the ocean. The ad emphasizes that the models showcased here are perfect for those seeking fun and adventure out of life. It demonstrates that the car is sporty, yet spacious enough to hold four passengers in addition to a sizeable amount of luggage.

Next, I would like to break into regional groups to discuss what each of you will do to prepare to air the ad by next month. Let's first take a short break and meet back here in ten minutes. Thank you.

解説

Introduction

感謝のことば、集合の目的 → キャンペーンの説明に使える!

Good morning, ladies and gentlemen. First of all, thank you all for making the effort to attend this meeting to discuss the start of our new advertising campaign "Drive on the edge!"(キャンペーン名) We will launch this campaign exactly one month from today using TV, radio and print media(媒体). This will be a full-scale, global campaign, targeting all English(使用言語)-speaking countries where our cars(製品) are sold. The target segment will be primarily single males and females from 25 to 35 who are looking to add some spice to their lives with a stylish, sporty automobile.(ターゲット層)

訳 皆さま、おはようございます。まずは、我々の新しい広告キャンペーン「ドライブ・オン・ザ・エッジ！」の開始にあたり、ミーティングを行なうためにお集まりいただきありがとうございます。このキャンペーンはテレビ、ラジオ、新聞、雑誌等で今日からちょうど1か月後にスタートします。これはわが社の車を販売している英語圏の国々すべてをターゲットとした本格的規模の世界的なキャンペーンとなります。今回の販売ターゲット層は主に25歳から35歳の独身男女で、スタイリッシュでスポーティな車を持つことで暮らしに刺激を加えたいと考えている人たちです。

Notes
- first of all … 「まず〜」。列挙が好きな英語は、first, second, third … と論理展開を番号で指し示すことが多い。
- attend this meeting 「会議に参加する」
- launch 「（キャンペーンを）開始する」。ご存知、ロケットの打ち上げにも使われる動詞。
- segment 分野、団体、対象など、ある「まとまり」を示す便利なビジネス用語。
- add some spice to … 「〜に刺激を加える」

Body

イメージの説明 → コマーシャルの説明に使える!

The TV commercial that will be used initially is currently in production and will be ready for the campaign launch date next month. It depicts a young female in her late 20s driving along a coastal highway with three friends in the car. They arrive at a beach, unload scuba equipment from the back, gear up and plunge into the ocean. The ad emphasizes that the models showcased here are perfect for those seeking fun and adventure out of life. It demonstrates that the car is sporty, yet spacious enough to hold four passengers in addition to a sizeable amount of luggage.

TOPIC 28 プロジェクト開始――ミーティングでの挨拶

| TOPIC 28 | プロジェクト開始――ミーティングでの挨拶

訳 最初に使われるテレビコマーシャルは現在製作が進んでおり、来月のキャンペーン開始時に間に合うように準備中です。このコマーシャルは20代後半の若い女性が3人の友達を乗せて海岸沿いの高速道路をドライブしているところから始まり、4人が海岸に到着し、スキューバの道具を車から降ろし、準備をして、海に飛び込むまでが映っています。ここに登場する車種は、日々の暮らしに楽しみやわくわくするような出来事を求めている人たちにふさわしいものであるとCMは描いています。そして、この車がスポーティで、それでいて大人4人とかなりの量の荷物を積めるだけの広さを持ったものであることを示しています。

Notes
- be in production 「製作中」
- be ready for … 「～に間に合う」。締め切りに間に合わせるのがビジネスの鉄則。
- depict 「描写する」。どのようなイメージかを説明する場合には、この単語を使いたい。
- unload 「降ろす」
- plunge into the ocean 「海に飛び込む」
- ad 「広告」。advertisement [advertising] の略。
- showcase 「登場する」

Conclusion
分科会、休憩をとる → 会議の司会に使える!

Next, I would like to break into regional（分科会の単位） groups to discuss what each of you will do to prepare to air the ad（業務内容） by next month. Let's first take a short break and meet back here in ten（休憩時間） minutes. Thank you.

訳 では次に、地域ごとに分かれて、それぞれが来月の広告の放送開始に向けてどのような準備を進めるか話し合っていただきたいと思います。10分ほどの休憩をはさんでまた集まってください。ありがとうございました。

Notes
- break into … 「～に分かれる」。グループ活動が盛んな国で便利な表現。
- air the ad 「広告を放送する」
- take a short break 「短い休憩をとる」といえば大体10分程度。

TOPIC 29 プロジェクト最新状況
——ミーティングでの挨拶

大手自動車会社のデザイナーが週次ミーティング開始の挨拶をします。

Track 29

Good morning, everybody. First on the agenda, I'd like to bring you up to date on what has been going on with the RX7 airbag project. Now that it is ready to enter design and testing, the R&D Division will be passing the torch on to us starting next week after they tie up a few loose ends.

Since I know that some of you are not quite up to speed on what has been happening with the project as of late, I'd like to take a few minutes to fill you in on recent events.

As you may have already heard, we hit a few snags with the preliminary design scheme during the R&D phase of the project. Basically, we had to scrap what we had as of two months ago and go back to square one due to a significant flaw in the inflation system design. This problem has since been rectified and we are now ready to create and test several prototypes.

You will all receive a detailed plan outlining the design and testing phase by the end of the week. Please review this before next Monday's meeting and be prepared to ask any questions you may have. Thank you.

解説

Introduction

最新状況の説明 → プロジェクトの進捗を説明するのに使える!

Good morning, everybody. First on the agenda, I'd like to bring you up to date on what has been going on with the RX7 airbag(製品名) project. Now that it is ready to enter design and testing(プロジェクト局面), the R&D(部署名) Division will be passing the torch on to us starting next week after they tie up a few loose ends.

> **訳** おはようございます、皆さん。議題の一番目ですが、RX7エアバッグ・プロジェクトについての最新情報をお伝えいたします。いよいよ設計とテストの段階になってまいりました。研究開発部門が最後の仕上げを完了し次第、来週中には我々にバトンを渡してくるはずです。

> **Notes**
> - first on the agenda 「議題の一番目の項目」。the first item on the agenda ということ。
> - bring you up to date on … 「〜の最新情報を伝える」
> - pass the torch on to … 下流工程の担当者に作業を任せること。torchは「たいまつ」の意味。
> - tie up a few loose ends ゆるんでいる箇所を締め上げる、つまり「仕上げを行なう」の意味。

Body 1

Body 2 のイントロ → 最新情報を伝える前置きに使える!

Since I know that some of you are not quite up to speed on what has been happening with the project as of late, I'd like to take a few minutes to fill you in on recent events.

> **訳** ここにいらっしゃる方の中には現在のプロジェクト状況を完全に把握していないこともあろうかと思うので、最近の動きについて少しお話ししましょう。

> **Notes**
> - be up to speed on … 「〜を把握している」
> - as of late 「現在の(状況)」
> - fill you in on … 「〜で満たす」、つまり「〜を知らせる」。通常は、最新状況の説明となる。

Body 2

プロジェクトのやり直し → プロマネなら使える！

As you may have already heard, we hit a few snags with the preliminary design scheme during the R&D(プロジェクト局面) phase of the project. Basically, we had to scrap what we had as of two months ago and go back to square one due to a significant flaw in the inflation system design(問題の箇所). This problem has since been rectified and we are now ready to create and test several prototypes.

> **訳** すでにお聞きになっているかと思いますが、今回のプロジェクトにおいては研究開発の仮設計の段階でいくつかの問題にぶつかりました。インフレーション・システム・デザインの重大な欠陥により、基本的には2か月前のものは捨てざるを得なくなり、もともとあったデザインに戻すことになります。欠陥は修正されて、いくつかの試作品を作り、試す準備も整いました。

> **Notes**
> - 次のケースなら使えます！
>   デザインのトラブル → トラブル解決 → 再開発 → 再テスト
> - snag 「思わぬ障害」。problem, obstacle, hurdleなどと並んで「問題」に直面する場合に使われる用語。
> - scrap 「捨てる」
> - go back to square one 「最初の状態に戻す」。チェスなどで反則などのため振り出しに戻ることから。squareはチェス盤の「ます目」の意味。
> - flaw 「欠陥」
> - rectify 「修正する」。たまには変わった単語を使うのも気分転換になろう。solve, resolveだけでは物足りない方へ。

Conclusion

資料を届ける → 作業依頼に使える！

You will all receive a detailed plan outlining the design and testing(プロジェクト局面) phase by the end of the week. Please review this before next Monday's(次回の会議の日取り) meeting and be prepared to ask any questions you may have. Thank you.

> **訳** 今週末には皆さんのお手元に設計とテストの具体的な計画が届くと思います。来週月曜日のミーティングまでに目を通していただき、質問を考えておいてください。ありがとうございました。

TOPIC 29

プロジェクト最新状況――ミーティングでの挨拶

> **Notes**
> - I will send … ではなく、you will receive … とすると丁寧な表現になる。
> - outline 「概要を説明する」
> - by the end of the week 「今週末までに」
> - be prepared to … 「～しておく」

TOPIC 30 プロジェクト完了
——結果報告

国際非営利開発機構の日本のプロジェクト・マネージャーが理事会において、最近インドネシアで行なわれた開発事業について、その結果報告をします。

Track 30

Good afternoon. I would like to take a few moments to briefly summarize Project Back to School, which was concluded last month. The project put over 1 billion yen of tsunami relief aid to work to rebuild elementary schools in the areas of Indonesia hardest hit by the recent disaster.

Over a period of 9 months, 23 contractors from Japan worked on a total of 19 school reconstruction projects. The extent of these projects ranged from repairing minor structural damage to rebuilding several schools from the ground up. It impacted over 8,000 children who are now able to return to school thanks to the project's success.

I had the opportunity to conduct site visits at several of the schools that were rebuilt. Photographs of these schools before and after the reconstruction are shown in your handouts. It is clear from the photos that this project has provided much needed assistance to the children living in these communities.

Last but not least, I would like to add that without the generosity of donors throughout the world this project would not have been possible. Thank you.

解説

Introduction
プロジェクトの説明 → プロジェクトのカットオフに使える!

Good afternoon. I would like to take a few moments to briefly summarize Project Back to School(プロジェクト名), which was concluded last month(プロジェクト終了時期). The project put over 1 billion yen(拠出金額) of tsunami relief aid to work to rebuild elementary schools in the areas of Indonesia hardest hit by the recent disaster(充当方法).

訳 こんにちは。ただ今より、先月完了いたしました"Project Back to School"について簡単にまとめたものをご報告したいと思います。このあいだの災害で大きな被害を受けたインドネシアの地域に小学校を再建するため、津波基金から10億円以上を充てました。

Notes
- take a few moments to … 「時間をさいて〜する」。聴衆の時間をとるのだからtakeを使う。
- briefly summarize 「簡単にまとめる」
- be concluded 「完了する」
- put over … 「〜を拠出する」
- hardest hit by … 「〜で大きな被害を受ける」

Body 1
プロジェクトの詳細説明 → プロマネなら使える!

Over a period of 9(プロジェクト期間) months, 23(請負業者の数) contractors from Japan worked on a total of 19 school reconstruction(業務内容) projects. The extent of these projects ranged from repairing minor structural damage(業務詳細内容) to rebuilding several schools from the ground up(業務詳細内容). It impacted over 8,000 children(プロジェクトの成果) who are now able to return to school(プロジェクトの成果) thanks to the project's success.

訳 9か月ものあいだに、日本から23の請負業者が計19の学校再建計画に携わりました。これらの計画は簡単な建物の損傷の修理から、いちから学校を建て直す、といったものまで幅広く行なわれました。このプロジェクトの成功のお陰で、8000人以上の子供たちがまた学校に通えるようになったのです。

Notes
- contractors 「請負業者」
- work on … プロジェクトに「参加する」には、participate in … ではなく、work on + プロジェクト、という構文を使う。

- range from A to B 「AからBの範囲にわたる」。幅広い様子を表わす。
- from the ground up 「いちから」。文字通りには「地面から上を」という意味。

Body 2

視察報告 → 写真を使った視察説明にぴったり!

I had the opportunity to conduct site visits at several of the schools(対象) that were rebuilt. Photographs of these schools before and after the reconstruction are shown in your handouts. It is clear from the photos that this project has provided much needed assistance to the children living in these communities (対象).

訳 私は再建設中の学校をいくつか見て回る機会に恵まれました。皆さんのお手元の資料にそれらの学校の再建前と再建後の様子が写っている写真があります。写真を見ればおわかりいただけますが、今回のプロジェクトではこの地域に住む子供たちに必要な援助を十分に行なえたと言えます。

Notes
- このパラグラフのロジックは次のようにまとめられる。
  視察をした → 写真を撮った → 写真を見てプロジェクトの意義がわかる
  しっかりしたロジックに基づいてパラグラフが構築されていることがおわかりいただけるだろう。

Conclusion

協力者への感謝 → 「〜なしでは…できなかったでしょう」の構文が使える!

Last but not least, I would like to add that without the generosity of donors(協力者) throughout the world this project would not have been possible. Thank you.

訳 最後になりましたが、世界中の国々から、多大なる寄付をいただいた方々なしには今回のプロジェクトの成功はなかったことを付け加えさせていただきます。ここに心より御礼申し上げます。

Notes
- Last but not least 「最後になりました (けっして軽んじているわけではない) が」。スピーチの決まり文句。暗記すること。
- donors 「寄付をしてくれた人」

TOPIC 30 プロジェクト完了——結果報告

TOPIC 31 調査結果の報告

大手自動車会社の安全テスト部門の責任者が、新しく開発したエアバッグの安全性について調査結果を報告します。

Track 31

We have completed our safety testing on the new RX7 airbag project, and I would like to report on our findings.

We subjected the airbag to a variety of tests, including head-on, rear-impact and side-impact collisions to measure deployment and durability. I will focus today on the results of the head-on collisions since they represent the most extreme conditions of an accident.

We simulated 50 high-speed collisions ranging from speeds of 25kph to 120kph. We are happy to report that the airbag inflated in 100% of the tests in 0.5 seconds or less. This is a 2% increase over the previous model's deployment ratio of 98%.

Regarding durability and impact sustainability, the RX7 was able to absorb the full force of a passenger load of up to 195kg in a 120kph collision.

The complete results of our testing can be accessed through the in-house shared directory under Safety Testing/RX7 Results. I'd be happy to address any questions you have at this time.

解説

Introduction

状況を知らせる

We have completed our safety testing on the new RX7 airbag (製品名) project, and I would like to report on our findings.

> 訳　新しいRX7エアバッグの安全性テストが終わりましたので、所見を報告します。

> Notes
> - complete our safety testing on … 「〜の安全性テストを完了する」
> - report on our findings 「テスト結果を報告する」。「〜について」には前置詞onを使う。findingsは、「（テストや調査の）結果」を指し、通常、複数形となる。

Body 1

実施したテスト内容を知らせる

We subjected the airbag to a variety of tests, including head-on, rear-impact and side-impact collisions to measure deployment and durability. I will focus today on the results of the head-on collisions since they represent the most extreme conditions of an accident.

> 訳　前方と後方、そして側面からの衝撃を含むさまざまなテストをして、エアバッグの膨らみ具合と耐久性を調査しました。本日は、事故時においてきわめて危険な状況となる、前方からの衝撃に対する結果を申し上げます。

> Notes
> - 技術的な内容のテストを種類に分け報告している。何種類もある中から、報告の対象となるテストを説明している。その場合、I will focus today on … と、focus on …（〜に焦点を合わせる）が使える。
> - subject 物 to … 「（物を）〜の対象とする」
> - deployment 「拡がること」。ここではエアバッグの膨らみ具合。
> - durability 「耐久性」
> - focus on … 「〜を中心に話す」
> - represent 「代表する」

Body 2

具体的なテスト結果について報告する

We simulated 50 high-speed collisions ranging from speeds of 25kph to 120kph. We are happy to report that the airbag inflated in 100% of the tests in 0.5 seconds or less. This is a 2% increase over the previous model's deployment ratio of 98%.

訳 時速25 kmから120 kmまでのあいだで50回の高速衝撃のシミュレーションを行ないました。0.5秒以下ですべてのエアバッグが膨張しました。前回のモデルの98%という割合を2%上回る結果です。

Notes
- ときとして、このパラグラフのような技術的なデータを発表に盛り込まなければいけないことがあるので、参考にされたい。
- simulate 「シミュレーションを行なう」
- be happy to report that … 「〜を報告できてうれしい」
- increase over … 「〜を上回る」

Body 3
別のテスト項目についての結果を報告する

Regarding durability and impact sustainability, the RX7 was able to absorb the full force of a passenger load of up to 195kg in a 120kph collision.

訳 耐久性と衝撃緩和性ですが、RX7は時速120 km時に195 kgまでの助手席に座っている人を支えることができました。

Notes
- regarding … 「〜に関して言えば」。with regard to …, concerning … と同義で、トピックを特定する。
- sustainability 「緩和性」
- up to … 「〜まで」

Conclusion
テスト結果閲覧の案内、質問をうながす

The complete results of our testing can be accessed through the in-house shared directory under Safety Testing/RX7 Results. I'd be happy to address any questions you have at this time.

訳 全テスト結果は社内共有ディレクトリ下、「セーフティ・テスティング／RX7結果」をご覧ください。何かご質問があれば、喜んでお答えいたします。

Notes
- I'd be happy to … 「喜んで〜する」
- address any questions ほかにも、entertain any questions, answer any questions がある。

TOPIC 32 ボーナスの報告

半導体関連機器メーカーの財務部長が、シリコンバレーにある米国支社の製造部門に対してボーナスの報告をします。

Track 32

I am pleased to announce that the numbers are in for 2006, and we had an excellent year. Sales worldwide were up 19%, while sales in the U.S. increased a whopping 24% over the previous year. In response to this, the manufacturing department did an excellent job of meeting this increase in demand from the sales department. Production times were cut by an average of 6% and defects were down by 5%. Congratulations!

To show our gratitude, we will be distributing bonuses in your next paycheck as follows. Employees hired since March 2005 will receive a bonus equivalent to 5% of annual salary. All other employees will receive 125% of the bonus amount received last year.

Without your wonderfully efficient work and careful attention to detail, we would not be able to produce our equipment fast enough to handle the rapidly growing number of orders we are receiving. We thank you for your hard work in hopes that you will provide us with even better performance results in 2007. Good job, everybody!

解説

Introduction

好業績報告 → 発表の表現に使える!

I am pleased to announce that the numbers are in for 2006(年), and we had an excellent year. Sales worldwide were up 19%(上昇率), while sales in the U.S.(国名) increased a whopping 24%(上昇率) over the previous year. In response to this, the manufacturing(部署名) department did an excellent job of meeting this increase in demand(状況) from the sales(部署名) department. Production times were cut by an average of 6(製造時間の削減)% and defects were down by 5(不良品発生の削減率)%. Congratulations!

訳 ここに2006年の数字をご報告いたしますが、今年は本当に素晴らしい年でした。世界各国での売上げ平均が19%の伸びを示した中で、米国での売上高はなんと前年比24％以上の伸びとなりました。この営業部からの需要に応えるべく、製造部門の皆さんもよくやってくださいました。製造時間は6％、不良品も5％削減することができました。おめでとうございます!

Notes
- 海外売上高 → 国内売上高 → 生産性（製造時間、不良品発生率）という流れ
- 基本形をおさえて、かつ表現のバリエーションをもたせる点に気をつけよう。

  ＜増＞   ＜減＞
  Sales were up … Sales were down …
  Defects increased … Defects decreased …

- the numbers are in 「数字があがっている」
- whopping 「途方もない」。whopは「強い衝撃」のこと。
- in response to … 「～に応える」
- production times 「製造時間」
- defects 「不良品」

Body

ボーナス支給

To show our gratitude, we will be distributing bonuses in your next paycheck as follows. Employees hired since March 2005(採用年月) will receive a bonus equivalent to 5(率)% of annual salary. All other employees will receive 125(率)% of the bonus amount received last year.

訳 ここに感謝の気持ちを込めて、皆さんの次の給料に次のようにボーナスが加算されることになりました。2005年3月以降から働いている皆さんには年俸の5％を、その他の従業員の皆さんには去年受け取ったボーナスの125％にあたる額が支払われます。

Notes
- show our gratitude 「感謝の気持ちを込める」
- distribute bonuses 「ボーナスを出す」
- paycheckは給料支払小切手。給料を銀行振り込みにするか、しないかは本人に任せられる。小切手は現金と同様の扱いとなるが、紛失しても再発行できる。
- equivalent to … 「〜に相当する」

Conclusion

感謝のことば → 「〜なしでは…できなかったでしょう」の構文

Without your wonderfully efficient work and careful attention to detail, we would not be able to produce our equipment(製品) fast enough to handle the rapidly growing number of orders we are receiving. We thank you for your hard work in hopes that you will provide us with even better performance results in 2007(年). Good job, everybody!

訳 皆さんがとても能率よく、また隅々まで気を配って仕事をしてくださったおかげで、あれだけ急増した受注に対応できました。2007年の結果もまた今年以上でありますよう、頑張ってください。皆さん、期待しています。

Notes
- 優れた業績に対する感謝のことばとして、そのまま使えるパラグラフである。
- handle orders 「受注に対応する」
- in hopes that … 「〜を願って」

※POINT

ボーナスのあるなし

今回のケースはボーナスが支給されるという場面です。日本の企業では毎年2回のボーナス支給が行なわれるのに対し、年俸制をとるような海外のケースではボーナスは「特別な報酬」として考えられる場合が多いようです。また、従業員一律のボーナス支給ではなく、優秀な成績をおさめた者に対して報酬を与えるケースの方が多いでしょう。個人が目立っても、周りはそれをよしとする考え方が広まっているからです。昇給についても同様のことがいえます。毎年昇給が期待できる、というわけではなく、昇給がない年もあります。私はかつて、数年にわたって昇給がなかったり、あってもインフレ調整程度だったりと、今から考えると悲惨な給与体系の下、アメリカで働いていました。またボーナスもたった1度だけもらった覚えがあります。でも、お昼1食分ぐらいでした。

TOPIC 32 ボーナスの報告

TOPIC 33 解雇の通達

大手金融機関の人事部長が従業員に向けて解雇の通達を行ないます。ヨーロッパと北米からの従業員が多くを占めています。

Track 33

Good afternoon, ladies and gentlemen.

I regret to say that it is not with good news that I stand before you today. We have been facing increasingly severe competition in our industry over the past two years. We have also recently lost a number of major clients to our competitors. As a result, we are now faced with having to take drastic action to stay in business. This will include reducing our payroll by 65 employees over the coming six months.

Deciding where to make these cuts is of course a very difficult decision. We value the services provided by each and every one of you. However, we unfortunately have no choice in this matter if we want to keep the company from going under.

Our first step will be to offer a voluntary early retirement package. Depending on how many choose this option, we will then decide by the end of March which jobs we will have to cut.

It is with my deepest regret that I make this announcement and I ask for your understanding and cooperation. Thank you.

解説

Introduction
挨拶

Good afternoon, ladies and gentlemen.

訳　皆さん、こんにちは。

Body 1
悪況、対策を説明するのに使える！

I regret to say that it is not with good news that I stand before you today. We have been facing increasingly severe competition in our industry over the past two years(競争が激化した時期). We have also recently lost a number of major clients to our competitors. As a result, we are now faced with having to take drastic action to stay in business. This will include reducing our payroll by 65 employees over the coming six months(対策).

訳　本日は、残念ながら皆さんに悪いニュースをお伝えしなければなりません。わが社はこの2年間、業界内の厳しい競争に直面してきました。また最近になって大口の取引先をいくつも他社に取られてしまいました。その結果、生き残りをかけて思い切った対策を取らなければならなくなりました。その1つとして、これから半年の間に従業員数を65人削減しなければなりません。

Notes
- regret to say that …　「残念ながら〜である」
- face severe competition　「厳しい競争に直面する」
- lose A to B　「BにAを奪われる」
- take drastic action　「思い切った対策を取る」
- stay in business　「経営を続ける」
- reduce our payroll　「給料を減らす」。ここでは「人員削減をする」という意味。

Body 2
決断が困難であることを伝えるのに使える！

Deciding where to make these cuts is of course a very difficult decision. We value the services provided by each and every one of you. However, we unfortunately have no choice in this matter if we want to keep the company from going under.

解雇の通達

> **訳** どの部署からカットしていくかの決断は非常に困難です。皆さんお一人おひとりのされている仕事はどれも価値あるものです。しかしながら、わが社が倒産をまぬがれるためには致し方ないことなのです。

Notes
- make these cuts 「削減する」
- each and every one of you 「一人ひとりの」という強調表現。
- have no choice … 個人、組織に選択の余地が与えられることが尊ばれる国では、「悪いこと」に関してよく使われる表現。
- going under = go bankrupt（倒産する）

Body 3
具体的な対策を提案する

Our first step will be to offer a voluntary early retirement package（対策名）. Depending on how many choose this option, we will then decide by the end of March（意思決定の期限）which jobs we will have to cut.

> **訳** まず初めに行ないますのが、早期退職者プログラムであります。どれだけの方がこのプログラムを受けられるかによりますが、3月末までにどの職種が対象になるかを決定したいと思います。

Notes
- early retirement package 「早期退職プログラム」。一般に自己都合による退職に比べ、退職金が多くもらえるようになっている。
- depending on … 「〜によるが」

Conclusion
残念な気持ちを述べるとともに、協力を乞う

It is with my deepest regret that I make this announcement and I ask for your understanding and cooperation. Thank you.

> **訳** このような発表をいたしますのは非常に残念ではありますが、どうぞご理解いただけますようお願い申し上げます。ありがとうございました。

Notes
- 好ましくない発表に使える文章。そのまま覚えたい。
- It is with my deepest regret that … 「〜は残念です」
- make this announcement 「発表する」

TOPIC 34 ブレーンストーミングでの挨拶

クリストファー・アーノルドは、インターネットでコマーシャル調査や宣伝を請け負う国際企業の制作部長です。今回、日本市場における新製品のためのアイディアについて、日本側の企業とブレーンストーミングを行ないます。

Track 34

Good morning. It's a pleasure to be back and to have the chance to meet with all of you in person. As I mentioned in the memo I sent last week, I would like to spend a few hours this morning generating ideas for new internet-based advertising products to introduce into the Japanese market.

I know that several of you have recently held focus groups with advertisers to discuss internet-based services they would like to see available on cell phones. I hope that this will provide us with some useful insight.

I think we should do this in the form of a brainstorming session. Once we begin, I'd like everybody to throw out any ideas that you have — good or bad, practical or impractical. At first I'm looking just for quantity, so don't hesitate to mention anything that comes to mind. Once we have a few dozen ideas on the table to consider, we'll go back over them one by one in more detail and discuss how feasible they might be.

Is that clear? OK, let's put our heads together and get some good ideas flowing. Who would like to begin?

解説

Introduction
再会を喜ぶ、ブレストの目的を説明する → 会議の司会に使える！

Good morning. It's a pleasure to be back and to have the chance to meet with all of you in person. As I mentioned in the memo I sent last week, I would like to spend a few hours this morning generating ideas for new internet-based advertising(製品の分野) products to introduce into the Japanese(市場とする国) market.

> **訳** おはようございます。今回また戻ってまいりまして、こうして皆さんにお会いできますことをうれしく思っています。先週お送りした覚書にも記したとおり、日本市場で売り出す新製品のインターネット上の広告についてのアイディアを出していただきたく、午前中に数時間をさきたいと思います。

> **Notes**
> - spend a few hours 「数時間」と言っているが、時間にさほど厳密になる必要はない。例えば、I'll be back in a second.（1秒後に戻ってくる）は、「すぐに」と読み代える。
> - generate ideas 「アイディアを出す」
> - … productsの業種をまたがった汎用表現はour products。以下、分野によって使い分ける。
>
> | 弊社製品 | our products |
> |---|---|
> | コンピュータ製品 | computer products |
> | 自動車製品 | automotive products |
> | バイオテクノロジー製品 | biotechnology products |
> | 化学製品 | chemical products |
> | オフィス家具 | office furniture products |
> | 乳製品 | dairy products |
> | 事務用品 | stationery products |
> | 農産物 | produce（productsではなく） |

Body 1
意見を求める

I know that several of you have recently held focus groups with advertisers(業者) to discuss internet-based(サービスの特徴) services they would like to see available on cell phones(媒体). I hope that this will provide us with some useful insight.

> **訳** 携帯電話でのインターネット上のサービスの可能性について広告主側と話し合いを持たれた方がいらっしゃるようですが、ぜひ活発なご意見をお聞かせください。

Notes
- hold focus groups 「フォーカス・グループを持つ」。一般的には「話し合いを持つ」と解釈できる。
- provide us with … 意見、資料の提供を求める際に便利な表現。provideは前置詞にwithをとり、"provide＋人＋with＋提供を求めているもの（=some useful insight)"となる。

Body 2

ブレストの手順の説明 → ブレストの簡易化に使える！

I think we should do this in the form of a brainstorming session. Once we begin, I'd like everybody to throw out any ideas that you have – good or bad, practical or impractical. At first I'm looking just for quantity, so don't hesitate to mention anything that comes to mind. Once we have a few dozen ideas on the table to consider, we'll go back over them one by one in more detail and discuss how feasible they might be.

訳 このミーティングは、ブレーンストーミングという形をとります。始まりましたら今お持ちのアイディアをなんでもいいですから、良いのも悪いのも、実用的なものもそうでないものも、出していただきたいと思います。まずは、できるだけたくさんのご意見を伺いたいので、思いつくものはどんどん仰ってください。かなりの数のアイディアが出揃ったところで、一つひとつについての具体的な検証に入り、実用化に向けての可能性を話し合っていきたいと思います。

Notes
- shouldは「義務」と覚えているかもしれないが、この場合のように「～しましょう」に近いニュアンスで使われることが多い。Let's … でも言い換えられる。
- in the form of … 「～の形で」
- throw out ideas 「アイディアを出す」
- look for quantity 「数を気にする」
- hesitateは英語圏の人がもっとも嫌う概念。何事にも「積極的な」態度が必要である。
- have … on the table 「～が出揃う」。文字通りは「テーブルに並べられる」という意味。
- feasible 「実用可能な」

TOPIC 34 ブレーンストーミングでの挨拶

Conclusion

理解したのを確認して、ブレストを開始する

Is that clear? OK, let's put our heads together and get some good ideas flowing. Who would like to begin?

訳 おわかりいただけましたか？ それでは、頭を寄せ集めて、いいアイディアを出していきましょう。どなたから始めていただきましょうか？

Notes
- put our heads together 「頭を寄せ合う」
- get some good ideas flowing 「知恵を絞る」

POINT

ブレストとは？

ブレーンストーミングは、できるだけ多くのアイディアを出し合うことを目的としています。恥ずかしいなどと思わずにアイディアを出すことが求められます。そのためには、発言の内容について、ブレーンストーム中は「批判しない」ことです。

独創性を養うためのブレストを教育に導入している場合があります。ここでも、発言の内容について、ブレーンストーム中は批判しないことが大切です。それを通して協調性を養い、共同作業を通してお互いの考え方を知ることができます。

出されたアイディアについては、実用化の検討をして、実施内容が決まったところで今後の作業分担を明確にしましょう。結果をうまくまとめて、作業分担を振り分けておかないと、単なる「井戸端会議」に終わってしまいかねません。

TOPIC 34 ブレーンストーミングでの挨拶

TOPIC 35 お知らせ
――ミーティングの最後に

ミーティングの最後に、伝達事項を説明します。LAN メンテナンス、考査、在宅勤務についてです。

Track 35

Before we wrap up, I'd like to go over some general announcements and housekeeping items.

First of all, the Systems Department will be conducting maintenance on the LAN tomorrow night, so the network will be down from 9 p.m. to midnight. This also means that you will not be able to log into the server from home to check your email during this time.

Our semi-annual reviews will be held starting next week. Most of you will be meeting with just me. The senior managers will meet with both me and Vice-President Swift. During the review, we will go over how well you have been accomplishing the annual objectives you set in January. We will also let you know if you are eligible for a pay increase and how much this will be.

Finally, many of you have been asking about the option of telecommuting several days a week. I've taken this up with senior-level management and am still waiting for their response. Since this type of policy has already been implemented in other divisions, I am optimistic that they will approve the request. I'll keep you posted.

That's it for now. Have a good day, everybody.

解説

Introduction

発表の用意

Before we wrap up, I'd like to go over some general announcements and housekeeping items.

訳 （会議を）終わらせる前に、全体への発表とお知らせを申し上げます。

Notes
- お知らせを発表する言い方が、特に参考になろう。状況としては、会議の最後に発表するということから、Before we wrap up … （会を終える前に）で始まっている。
- go over … 「～を説明する」
- housekeeping items 「社内のお知らせ事項」

Body 1

メンテナンスの予定

First of all, the Systems Department will be conducting maintenance on the LAN tomorrow night, so the network will be down from 9 p.m. to midnight 〈ダウンする時間〉. This also means that you will not be able to log into the server from home to check your email during this time.

訳 始めに、システム部が明日の夜、LANのメンテナンスを行なうので、午後9時から12時までネットワークがダウンします。このため、この時間帯に自宅からEメールをチェックしようと思っても、サーバーにログインできません。

Notes
- 次の流れで発表がなされている。
  メンテナンスの対象（maintenance on the LAN）→ ダウンする時間（down from … to ～）→ 影響（not be able to …）
- log into the server 「サーバーへログインする」
- check your email 「Eメールをチェックする」

Body 2

考査の予定

Our semi-annual reviews will be held starting next week. Most of you will be meeting with just me. The senior managers will meet with both me and Vice-President Swift. During the review, we will go over how well you have been accomplishing the annual objectives you set in January. We will also let you know if you are eligible for a pay increase and how much this will be.

> **訳** 半年に一度の考査を来週から始めます。ほとんどの皆さんは私とだけ面談をします。専務取締役は、私とスウィフト副社長の両方と面談することになります。考査では、皆さんが1月に掲げた年間目標をどれだけ達成できたかを振り返ってみます。また昇給が望めるか、望めるならどのくらいなのかをお伝えします。

> **Notes**
> - 年間目標をどの程度達成できたか（how well you have been accomplishing the annual objectives）が考査（reviews）の焦点となる。このケースでは、その結果によって、昇給（a pay increase）が決まってくるらしい。
> - be eligible for … 「～の対象となる」

Body 3
在宅勤務の行方

Finally, many of you have been asking about the option of telecommuting several days a week. I've taken this up with senior-level management and am still waiting for their response. Since this type of policy has already been implemented in other divisions, I am optimistic that they will approve the request. I'll keep you posted.

> **訳** 最後に、多くの皆さんが週に数日の在宅勤務を希望していらっしゃいますが、この件につきましては、取締役会に上げましたので、報告待ちの状態です。このような方法はすでに他の部署では実行されていますので、ここでもご要望にお応えできるのではと楽観視しています。経過は追ってご報告します。

> **Notes**
> - コンピュータ業界では珍しくないが、今では在宅勤務（telecommuting）を許可している会社もある。commuteは「通勤する」、tele-は「遠隔」という意味なので、自宅で通信を使った勤務を指す。
> - take this up with … 「～に話を持ちかける」
> - wait for their response 「回答を待つ」

Conclusion
終わりのことば

That's it for now. Have a good day, everybody.

> **訳** 以上です。では皆さん、今日も一日頑張ってください。

> **Notes**
> - 会議の終わりにする発表なので、終わりのことばは短めにしたい。
> - That's it for now. 「以上です」。That's it. だけでも使われる。

TOPIC 36 会社の社会奉仕について説明する

大手製薬会社の地域活動部長が年次国際支援者総会にて会社の社会奉仕についての概要を説明します。

Track 36

Good afternoon. I would like to give an overview of our social contributions made in 2005. In accordance with our corporate philosophy of "Helping to build strong communities", we have pioneered a number of philanthropic community outreach programs.

Our "Centers for Seniors" program contributed over ¥10 million for the construction of senior citizen community centers in rural areas of Japan. We also helped organize a number of community volunteer programs to provide staffing assistance for these centers.

As Japan's elderly population continues to grow, there is an increasing demand for health care workers in the area of senior citizen care. To help meet these demands, we have set up scholarship funds at 12 nursing schools throughout the country. We disbursed over ¥75 million in scholarships in 2005 to deserving students specializing in elderly care.

Finally, on an international level, we responded to the recent natural disasters in Southeast Asia by providing over ¥3 million in medical supplies to assist the tsunami and earthquake victims in Indonesia and Pakistan in 2005.

As you can see, we take the idea of corporate social responsibility to heart, helping communities to help us build a better world.

解説

Introduction

始めのことば、活動について

Good afternoon. I would like to give an overview of our social contributions made in 2005(年度). In accordance with our corporate philosophy of "Helping to build strong communities", we have pioneered a number of philanthropic community outreach programs.

> **訳** こんにちは。2005年のわが社の社会奉仕について説明させていただきます。私どもは「地域社会の強い結びつきに貢献すること」という企業哲学により、さまざまな慈善地域活動を率先して行なっています。

> **Notes**
> - give an overview of … 「~の概要を説明する」
> - In accordance with … 「~により」
> - pioneer 「~を率先して行なう」
> - corporate philosophyは、企業が経営を行なう上での哲学を表わしたもの。そのほか、corporate principle（理念）やcorporate strategies（戦略）がある。communityという概念は、あまり日本では知られていない。ビジネスの中心である大都市にはcommunityという考え方は案外希薄であるが、最近では見直されてきた考え方のひとつだろう。

Body 1

具体的な地域活動の紹介

Our "Centers for Seniors" program contributed over ¥10 million(金額) for the construction of senior citizen community centers in rural areas of Japan. We also helped organize a number of community volunteer programs to provide staffing assistance for these centers.

> **訳** 「シニア・センター」プログラムにより、国内の農村地帯に住む高齢者のためのコミュニティー・センター設立に1000万円が費やされました。また、こういった施設で働くスタッフを派遣する、さまざまな地域ボランティア組織の応援も行なってきました。

> **Notes**
> - contributedとは、「寄付を行なった」ということ。「貢献」という概念的なものにとどまらず、企業ではやはり「資金」を指す場合が多い。
> - organize a program 「プログラム（活動）をとりまとめる」

TOPIC 36 会社の社会奉仕について説明する

Body 2
具体的な地域活動の紹介（続き）

As Japan's elderly population continues to grow, there is an increasing demand for health care workers in the area of senior citizen care. To help meet these demands, we have set up scholarship funds at 12(数) nursing schools throughout the country. We disbursed over ¥75 million(金額) in scholarships in 2005(年度) to deserving students specializing in elderly care.

訳 日本の高齢者人口の増加に伴い、シニア・センターで働く介護者の需要は年々増えています。この需要に応えるために、わが社では国内12の介護者養成学校に奨学金を支給しています。2005年には高齢者介護専攻の優秀な学生に対し、計7500万円以上の奨学金を支給しました。

Notes
- 「奨学金」という形で寄付を行なうことがある。最後の2文を参考にして、自分のケースに書き換えていただきたい。基本形は次のとおり。
    We have set up scholarship funds at …
    We disburse over … in scholarships
- elderly population 「高齢者人口」
- health care 「介護」
- meet these demands 「需要に応える」
- deserving 「優秀な」。本来の意味は「奨学金をもらうに値する」。

Body 3
具体的な地域活動の紹介（続き）

Finally, on an international level, we responded to the recent natural disasters(災害) in Southeast Asia(地域) by providing over ¥3 million(金額) in medical supplies(使途) to assist the tsunami and earthquake victims in Indonesia and Pakistan(国名) in 2005(年度).

訳 最後になりましたが、わが社の国際的な活動として、最近の東南アジアでの自然災害時に、2005年にインドネシアとパキスタンの津波、地震の被害者への医療品供給に300万円以上の援助をいたしました。

Notes
- 近頃では、地域を国内に限定せず、国外にも適用する考え方が広く見られる。このパラグラフでは、実際にあった話題を参考にしている。
- respond to … 「～へ対応する」
- medical supplies 「医療品供給」

Conclusion
結びのことば

As you can see, we take the idea of corporate social responsibility to heart, helping communities to help us build a better world.

訳 ご覧いただいていますように、地域社会でのこうした活動がよりよい社会を作っていくという、企業の社会的責任を肝に銘じていきたいと思います。

Notes
- take … to heart 「真剣に〜を考える」
- corporate social responsibility 「CSR」として広く知られている。

TOPIC 37 朝礼の挨拶

東京のグラフィック・デザイン会社であるインターナショナル・デザイン・デパートメント・オブ・ヴィスオで朝礼が行なわれています。

🎵 Track 37

Good morning, everybody. First off, kudos to all of you who stayed late last night working on the RWB project. I received confirmation this morning that the first set of proofs should be back for our review on Thursday.

Next, let's go over today's schedule. I'd like to have Shotaro and Klara focus on the MobileMedia project. Let's try to have a draft of their logo ready to go out the door by 3 so that sales can take it over for their approval by COB. The text files for the New Star Hotel pamphlet are back from translation, so I'd like to see Trish and Emiko work on the text layout. Can you wrap up a draft by 5? Finally, I'd like to ask Peter and Kuan-Yin to work on getting all the text in place for the Chinese version of the Supernova Communications website.

Also, Mark called in sick with the flu this morning and may be out for a few days.

I'll be tied up in a managers' meeting for most of the morning, but will be in my office this afternoon if anything comes up.

Unless there are any questions, that's all I have. Thanks.

解説

Introduction
労をねぎらう

Good morning, everybody. First off, kudos to all of you who stayed late last night working on the RWB(プロジェクト名) project. I received confirmation this morning that the first set of proofs(作業事項) should be back for our review on Thursday(期限).

訳 皆さん、おはようございます。まずは、昨晩RWBプロジェクトで残業していた皆さん、大変ご苦労様でした。今朝、確認が取れましたが、初校（＝最初の校正刷り）が木曜日に出るそうです。

Notes
- 働きバチは日本人だけ、というのは神話。どこの世界にも働き者はいる。
- first off, … 「まずは〜」
- kudos to all of you 「皆さん、ご苦労様」
- work on … 「〜の仕事をする」。前置詞がonになるのは、なかなか思いつかない。
- receive confirmation that … 「〜という確認を受ける」

Body 1
スケジュールと役割の確認

Next, let's go over today's schedule. I'd like to have Shotaro and Klara(名前) focus on the MobileMedia(プロジェクト名) project. Let's try to have a draft of their logo(作業事項) ready to go out the door by 3(期限) so that sales can take it over for their approval by COB. The text files for the New Star Hotel pamphlet(作業事項) are back from translation, so I'd like to see Trish and Emiko(名前) work on the text layout. Can you wrap up a draft by 5(期限)? Finally, I'd like to ask Peter and Kuan-Yin(名前) to work on getting all the text in place for the Chinese(言語) version of the Supernova Communications(会社名) website.

訳 次に、本日の予定です。正太郎とクララにはモービルメディアのプロジェクトに集中してもらいます。ロゴのドラフトを3時までに用意できれば、営業の方で5時までに承認をもらってきます。ニュースター・ホテルのパンフレットのテキストファイルが翻訳部門から上がってくるので、トリッシュと恵美子でレイアウトを考えてください。5時までにドラフトを仕上げられそうですか？それから最後に、ピーターとクァン・イン、スーパーノバ・コミュニケーションのウェブサイトの中国語訳をすべてお願いします。

TOPIC 37 朝礼の挨拶

Notes
- go over today's schedule 「スケジュールの確認をする」
- have ＋人＋ do 「人に〜をしてもらう」
  丁寧さの順で並べる。
    I would like to have you …
    I would like you to …
    I want you to …
- by COB 「営業時間終了までに」。Close Of Business のアクロニム（頭字語）。
- wrap up ＝ go out the door 「ドアから出る」、つまり「完成して発送できる状態にする」。

Body 2
病欠の従業員の様子を知らせる

Also, Mark(名前) called in sick with the flu this morning and may be out for a few days.

訳 また先ほどマークから連絡が入り、インフルエンザにかかったようなので、数日間休むそうです。

Notes
- flu は「インフルエンザ」。単なる「風邪」とは違うのは、ご存知のとおり。
- be out 「休みをとる」

Conclusion
自分の予定を告げる

I'll be tied up in a managers' meeting for most of the morning, but will be in my office this afternoon if anything comes up.

Unless there are any questions, that's all I have. Thanks.

訳 午前中、私は部長会議に出ていますが、午後は部屋にいますので、何かあったら来てください。

質問がなければ、これで終わりにします。ありがとう。

Notes
- be tied up 「縛られる」、つまり「忙しい」ということ。
- that's all I have. 「これで終わり」

TOPIC 38 株主総会 I
―― 株価動向

日本の半導体製造機器メーカー、セミコンの会長が、2005年の会社の株について株主総会で話します。

Track 38

Good morning, ladies and gentlemen. Welcome to the annual Semiqon shareholders' meeting. Let me begin with a quick overview of our stock performance in 2005.

In looking at the big picture, Semiqon started the year at 6,420 yen per share and closed out the year at 7,350 yen per share. This is an overall gain of over 14% for the year. Our stock peaked at 7,540 on October 4 and hit its low for the year of 5,880 on May 9. We paid dividends of 60 yen per share on March 20. Currently, we have 34,520,000 shares of outstanding common stock.

We had one major turn of events this year, which was our merger with Japan Electra. The merger deal was announced on May 15 and was the spark we needed to jump start our stock, which had been lingering below the 6,000-yen mark for several months up to that point. Once the merger plans solidified and were executed smoothly, our stock climbed steadily throughout the rest of the year.

We are expecting a continued rise in our stock price in 2006, and we hope to break 7,700 yen by the end of the first quarter.

解説

Introduction

株主総会開会宣言

Good morning, ladies and gentlemen. Welcome to the annual Semiqon(会社名) shareholders' meeting. Let me begin with a quick overview of our stock performance in 2005(年度).

訳 ここにお集まりの皆さま、おはようございます。セミコンの年次株主総会へようこそいらっしゃいました。まず始めに、2005年のわが社の株価動向について簡単にご説明させていただきます。

Notes
- shareholders' meeting 「株主総会」
- let me begin with … 「～から始めさせていただきます」。始めのことばのなかで、締めのことばとして決まり文句となっているので、いろいろな場面で応用が利く。
- a quick overview of … 「～の概略説明」
- stock performance 「株価動向」

Body 1

株価実績の説明

In looking at the big picture, Semiqon(会社名) started the year at 6,420 yen(年初株価) per share and closed out the year at 7,350 yen(年度末株価) per share. This is an overall gain of over 14(上昇率)% for the year. Our stock peaked at 7,540(株価最高値) on October 4(最高値をつけた日) and hit its low for the year of 5,880(株価最安値) on May 9(最安値をつけた日). We paid dividends of 60 yen(配当金) per share on March 20(配当支払日). Currently, we have 34,520,000(株式出来高) shares of outstanding common stock.

訳 大まかに見ますと、セミコン株は1株6420円で始まり、7350円で終わりました。総合的に見て年間14％の上昇となりました。年間最高値は10月4日に付けた7540円で、最安値は5月9日の5880円でした。3月20日に1株60円の配当金を支払わせていただきました。現在、発行済み普通株は34,520,000株です。

Notes
- 次の順序で説明がなされている。
  期首の株価 → 期末の株価 → 株価の上昇率 → 最高値 → 最安値 → 配当金 → 株数
  パターンが決まっているので、このパラグラフを参考に自社のケースに言い換えると練習になるだろう。

- look at the big picture 「大まかに見る」
- per share 「一株あたり」
- close out 「終値をつける」
- gain 「(株価)上昇」
- peak at … 「〜で最高値をつける」
- hit its low 「最安値をつける」
- pay dividends of … 「(価格〜の)配当金を支払う」
- outstanding common stock 「発行済み普通株」

Body 2

合併による株価への影響の説明

We had one major turn of events this year, which was our merger with Japan Electra(合併相手の名前). The merger deal was announced on May 15(合併が発表された日) and was the spark we needed to jump start our stock, which had been lingering below the 6,000-yen(株価) mark for several months up to that point. Once the merger plans solidified and were executed smoothly, our stock climbed steadily throughout the rest of the year.

訳 今年はわが社に大きな変化がありました。それはジャパン・エレクトラとの合併です。合併の話は5月15日に発表され、それまで数か月間5000円台後半の値動きに終始していた株価が、合併の話を機に急に活気を見せ始めました。合併計画が固まり、無事に施行されると、年末までの期間、わが社の株価は着実に値上がりしていきました。

Notes
- 昨今では買収、合併が盛んに行なわれているので、このパラグラフはそのような状況を説明するのに最適である。
  次の順序で説明されている。
  合併した企業名 → 合併の発表日 → 株価への影響
- have major turn of events 「大きな変化がある」
- merger with … 「〜との合併」
- spark 「契機」
- linger 「停滞する」
- solidify 「はっきり決まる」

TOPIC 38 株主総会 I ― 株価動向

Body 3

株価への今後の期待

We are expecting a continued rise in our stock price in 2006(年度), and we hope to break 7,700 yen(株価) by the end of the first quarter.

訳 2006年も引き続き株価の値上がりがありますように、第1四半期の終わりには7700円を上回るように期待しております。

Notes
- 一般的発言にとどまらず、今後の株価に対する具体的な期待に言及して終われば、効果的なスピーチになろう。
- break … 「～に達する」

TOPIC 39 株主総会 II
──合併のお知らせ

(TOPIC 38 の続き) 日本の半導体製造機器メーカー、セミコンの会長が、2005 年に行なわれた会社の合併について株主に話をします。

Track 39

Next, I would like to give some more detail on our merger with Japan Electra. To provide some background on the timeline, discussions on the subject began back in December of 2004. We hammered out the details throughout the spring and announced the merger to the press in May. The execution phase of the merger took place over the summer and was wrapped up for the most part by September.

As part of the agreement, we have maintained the name Semiqon since it already enjoys a high level of brand recognition worldwide. Combined with the former Japan Electra, we own and operate a total of seven production facilities in Japan, China and India with over 5,700 employees. Our assets total just over ¥13 billion and our domestic market share is now 17.4%.

As a result of the merger, we were able to pool our assets and expertise in semiconductor production equipment to become the fifth largest manufacturer in the industry in Japan.

The merger also had a positive impact on our stock price, which pulled out of a steady decline just after the official announcement in May and has been on the rise ever since.

解説

Body 4

合併の詳細説明

Next, I would like to give some more detail on our merger with Japan Electra (合併の会社名). To provide some background on the timeline, discussions on the subject began back in December of 2004 (年月). We hammered out the details throughout the spring and announced the merger to the press in May (月). The execution phase of the merger took place over the summer (合併時期) and was wrapped up for the most part by September (合併完了月).

訳 次にジャパン・エレクトラとの合併についてもう少し詳しくお話しいたします。時系列的にご説明いたしますと、2004年の12月に合併についての話し合いが始まりました。2005年の春いっぱいに詳細を詰め、5月に報道機関への発表を行ないました。実際の合併は夏のあいだに始まり、9月にはほとんど終了いたしました。

Notes
- 合併検討に関しての時期を説明する（provide some background on the timeline …）
- 話し合い（discussions）→ 詳細（details）→ 発表（announce）
  → 執行（execution）→ 終局（wrap up）
  話し合いが始まる（discussions on the subject began …）
  詳細について検討する（hammered out the details …）
  報道機関へ発表する（announced the merger to the press …）
  執行の局面を迎える（The execution phase of the merger took place …）
  合併を迎える（was wrapped up …）

Body 5

合併後の会社概要

As part of the agreement, we have maintained the name Semiqon (会社名) since it already enjoys a high level of brand recognition worldwide. Combined with the former Japan Electra (合併前の会社名), we own and operate a total of seven (生産拠点の数) production facilities in Japan, China and India (国名) with over 5,700 (従業員数) employees. Our assets total just over ¥13 billion (資産) and our domestic market share is now 17.4 (国内市場シェア率)%.

訳 合併契約の一部として、すでに世界的に認知度が高くなっていたセミコンという社名をそのまま残すことに合意いたしました。前ジャパン・エレクトラ社と合わせて、我々は現在日本国内、中国、そしてインドに7つの製

造工場を保有し、5700人の従業員を抱えています。わが社の総資産は130億円、国内マーケット・シェアは現在17.4%となっております。

Notes
- 次の順序で説明がなされている。
  企業名 → 工場数 → 従業員数 → 資本金 → 国内シェア

Body 6
合併後の業界での会社規模

As a result of the merger, we were able to pool our assets and expertise in semiconductor production equipment to become the fifth(順位) largest manufacturer in the industry in Japan(国名).

訳 合併の結果、2社の資産と半導体製造機器に関する専門技術を合わせ、国内業界第5位の規模のメーカーとなりました。

Notes
- pool our assets and expertise 「資産と専門技術を合わせる」。poolは「寄せ集める」という意味。「水たまり（pool）」は、雨水の「寄せ集め」である。

Body 7
合併の株価への影響

The merger also had a positive impact on our stock price, which pulled out of a steady decline just after the official announcement in May(月) and has been on the rise ever since.

訳 合併はわが社の株価にも好材料に働き、5月の公式発表後のじりじりした売りがその後、値上がりに向かっています。

Notes
- have a positive impact on … 「〜に良い影響が働く」。この反対の「悪い影響」は、negative impactとなる。
- pull out of … 「〜から抜け出す」
- be on the rise 「値上がりに向かう」
- 株価の動向は、「上昇（increase）」、「下降（decrease）」、「横ばい（stay the same）」の3つが基本である。

TOPIC 40 株主総会 Ⅲ
――株式分割のお知らせ

(TOPIC 39 の続き）日本の半導体製造機器メーカー、セミコンの会長が、株主に対して来る株式分割について話します。

Track 40

Finally, I would like to announce plans we have in the pipeline for a stock split next month. It will be a two-for-one split on our common stock. We are tentatively planning the split to take place on April 3 of this year, barring any snags in the final steps for approval from the Board of Directors.

On the day of the split, the quantity of common shares held by stockholders will double and the value of each share will be reduced by half. This will be our third stock split since going public in May 1999.

There are two main reasons that have prompted this stock split. First, we would like to increase the number of investors in Semiqon by lowering the minimum amount required to purchase our stock. This will make it more affordable and attractive to a wider range of individual investors.

Second, we hope that by reducing our share price to half of its current value to attract new investors, we will be able to create even more growth potential for the value of the stock. We expect to see a surge in the stock price immediately following the split, followed by stable growth throughout the rest of the year.

I'll be happy now to answer any questions you might have. Thank you.

解説

Body 8
株価分割の方針

Finally, I would like to announce plans we have in the pipeline for a stock split next month(時期). It will be a two-for-one(分割比) split on our common stock. We are tentatively planning the split to take place on April 3(日付) of this year, barring any snags in the final steps for approval from the Board of Directors.

訳 それでは最後に、準備中であります来月の株式分割の計画についてご説明させていただきます。今回、1：2の普通株式分割を行ないます。取締役会での最終承認に何の問題もなければ、4月3日に分割を行なう予定でいます。

Notes
- in the pipeline 「準備中で」
- two-for-one 「1つで2つの」。1株につき2株得ることができる、という意味。forの前と後で意味を取り違えないように。
- tentatively 「今のところ」
- bar any snags 「障害、問題を防ぐ」

Body 9
株価分割の内容

On the day of the split, the quantity of common shares held by stockholders will double and the value of each share will be reduced by half. This will be our third stock split since going public in May 1999(年月).

訳 分割当日、株主の皆さまのお持ちになっている株数は2倍になり、株価は半分になります。今回の株価分割は1999年5月に株式公開して以来3度目になります。

Notes
- go public 「株式公開する」。「公に行く」ということから、株式では「市場取引される」という意味になる。

Body 10
株式分割の理由

There are two main reasons that have prompted this stock split. First, we would like to increase the number of investors in Semiqon(会社名) by lowering the minimum amount required to purchase our stock. This will make it more affordable and attractive to a wider range of individual investors.

TOPIC 40

株主総会Ⅲ ── 株式分割のお知らせ

> **訳** 株式分割を行なうことの主な理由に次の2つを挙げたいと思います。1つ目は、株価購買における最低必要額を下げることでセミコンの投資家数を増やしたいということです。これで、セミコン株が今までよりさらに多くの個人投資家にとって買いやすく、魅力的になるはずです。

> **Notes**
> - 投資家の数を増やす（increase the number of investors）← 1株あたりの株価が下がれば、購入できる人が増える。
> - prompt … 「〜をするに至る」
> - affordable "afford" は「購入するだけの資金がある」という意味。
>   （例）I can't afford it.（とてもじゃないが、買えない）

Body 11
株式分割の理由

Second, we hope that by reducing our share price to half of its current value to attract new investors, we will be able to create even more growth potential for the value of the stock. We expect to see a surge in the stock price immediately following the split, followed by stable growth throughout the rest of the year.

> **訳** 2つ目の理由ですが、株価を現在の半値にすることで、新たな投資家を引き付け、株価の更なる値上がりの可能性を生み出せる、ということです。分割直後の株価の値上がり、そしてその後年末までの安定した値上がりを期待しています。

> **Notes**
> - 株価上昇への方策
> - see a surge in the stock price … 「上昇（surge）」を示す表現にはたくさんあるが、基本は up, increase であることを忘れないでいたい。

Conclusion
質問をうながす

I'll be happy now to answer any questions you might have. Thank you.

> **訳** では、これから皆さまからのご質問にお答えいたします。どうもありがとうございました。

TOPIC 41 四半期報告

日本の飛行機部品製造会社のカナダにある子会社の経理部長が、取締役会で四半期の財務報告をします。

Track 41

Good afternoon, ladies and gentlemen. I would like to present the highlights of our third-quarter financial data.

Net earnings were down 4% compared to the previous quarter to $16 million. This represents a value of $0.17 per share, off from the previous quarter's posting of $0.20 per share. Net sales dropped this quarter to an all-time low for the year of $157 million. This is down from our first-quarter peak of $169 million.

The decline of these numbers can be mostly attributed to both the sluggish economy and a decrease in the number of orders for airplanes received this quarter by the major players in the industry. With the financial situation of many North American airlines looking grim, we are not sure if we will be able to turn things around anytime soon.

Our outlook for fourth quarter is not optimistic. We are predicting that sales will continue to slide into the winter months. As a result, it may be necessary to resort to layoffs starting in the first quarter of the new year. While we should try to avoid this at all costs, it may be our only option if business does not begin to pick up soon.

解説

TOPIC 41 四半期報告

Introduction
四半期報告の始めのことば

Good afternoon, ladies and gentlemen. I would like to present the highlights of our third-quarter(四半期名) financial data.

> **訳** 皆さま、おはようございます。第3四半期財務資料の中で目立った点をご報告させていただきます。

> **Notes**
> - first, second, third, fourthでそれぞれ四半期を言い分ける。quarterはご存知だろうが、「4分の1」の意味。
> - 日本語では「ハイライトをお届けする」というが、英語ではそのままpresent the highlights of … となる。

Body 1
業績を説明する

Net earnings were down 4(下降率)% compared to the previous quarter to $16 million(純収益). This represents a value of $0.17(株価) per share, off from the previous quarter's posting of $0.20(株価) per share. Net sales dropped this quarter to an all-time low for the year of $157 million(売上高). This is down from our first-quarter peak of $169 million(売上高).

> **訳** 純収益は前期に比べまして4%の減少となり1600万ドルでした。これにより、前期の表記株価の0.20ドルを下回り、1株0.17ドルとなりました。今期の純売上高も過去最低のレベルにまで落ち、1億5700万ドルでした。これは、第1四半期の最高売上高1億6900万ドルから比べるとずいぶん低い数字になりました。

> **Notes**
> - 上昇、減少率で表わす会社業績は、すべて前期（前年）との比較となる。業績を数値で表わすには、次のような定型表現を使い分ける。日本語と違い、英語は同じ意味でもさまざまな表現を使うことが求められるので、同じ表現を繰り返し使わないように注意。
>   down 〜 % compared to …
>   up 〜 % compared to …
>   off from …
>   up from …
> - net earnings 「純利益」
> - $0.17　読み方は seventeen cents.
> - net sales 「純売上高」
> - all-time 「過去」「これまでで一番の」

Body 2
業績不振の背景分析

The decline of these numbers can be mostly attributed to both the sluggish economy and a decrease in the number of orders for airplanes(製品) received this quarter by the major players in the industry. With the financial situation of many North American airlines(業界) looking grim, we are not sure if we will be able to turn things around anytime soon.

> **訳** これら数値の低下は主に、景気後退と業界大手からの今期の飛行機部品受注の減少によるものです。多くの北米飛行機会社の財務状況が思わしくない現在、今の状態が好転するのには時間がかかりそうです。

> **Notes**
> - attributeとは、問題の原因となる現象を指すことば。そのほかの問題をも考えると、状況改善（turn things around）があるかも不明。
> - sluggish economy 「景気後退」
> - look grim 「(財務状況)が思わしくない」

Conclusion
次の四半期への展望と課題

Our outlook for fourth(期) quarter is not optimistic. We are predicting that sales will continue to slide into the winter(季節) months. As a result, it may be necessary to resort to layoffs starting in the first quarter of the new year(時期). While we should try to avoid this at all costs, it may be our only option if business does not begin to pick up soon.

> **訳** 第4四半期も楽観視できません。冬期に向けて、売上げはますます不調になると予想しています。その結果、来年第1四半期からレイ・オフを始めなければならないでしょう。これは何としても避けたいものですが、商況が早めに好転しなければ、わが社にとっての唯一の選択になると思います。

> **Notes**
> - outlook for … 「～の概況」
> - resort to … 「～に頼る」
> - at all costs 「何としても」
> - if business does not begin to pick up 「ビジネスが回復し始めないと」。pick upという動詞句がピンとこないかもしれないが、ビジネスが回復する状況を表わしている。

索 引
INDEX

あ行

アイディアを出す	146, 147
相手を理解する	65
頭を寄せ合う	148
(〜に)アップグレードする	100
(〜の)安全性テストを完了する	137
Eメールと電話でのやりとり	119
Eメールをチェックする	150
(〜を)生き抜く	75
以上です	151
以前の状態に戻る	77
忙しい	158
いただきます	65
いちから	135
一貫して成長を遂げる	58
一考に値する	101
1分間に〜の	101
一歩を踏み出す	75
いつも	54
今のところ	167
請負業者	134
疑いなく〜	62
疑いなく〜する	68
(BにAを)奪われる	143
売上高が減少した	77
上回る	85, 138
営業時間	47
営業時間外	97
営業時間終了までに	158
(〜から)得る	104
遠慮せず〜してください	38
(〜に)応募する	116
大きな変化がある	161
多くの人に会う	60
大まかに見る	161
(…は〜の)おかげによる	70
置き場所を節約できる	101
落ち着く	103
(〜を)お願いする	58
思い切った対策を取る	143
おもてなし	121
思わぬ障害	131
(〜に)お別れを告げる	53
終値をつける	161
恩師	71

か行

会議に参加する	127
(〜の)概況	171
介護	154
(人が)会社に勤めて6年になる	40
外敵に対して	81
回答を待つ	151
(〜に関する)概要を説明する	50
(〜の)概略説明	160
(AをBで)代える	75
顔をつき合わせて	119
革新的な	70
(〜という)確認を受ける	157
下降	165
(〜との)合併	161
合併で生まれる	88
稼働して	115
かなり仕事の量が減らされる	108
(〜の)可能性を考慮する	88
(株価)上昇	161
株価動向	160
株式公開する	167
株主	58
株主総会	160
我慢する	78
(〜するよう)駆られる	78
為替相場	77
変わらぬ信頼	58
観客が自由に〜できる	91
感激する	74
感謝の気持ちを込める	141
鑑賞する	64

完成して発送できる状態にする	158
簡単な概要	46
簡単にまとめる	134
乾杯する	65
(〜の)機会をもてる	33
危機から脱する	80
企業哲学は〜です	93
帰国する	34
(人に)期待する	44
軌道に乗る	115
機能して	115
厳しい競争に直面する	143
厳しい状況	57
厳しい手順を開発する	93
(キャンペーンを)開始する	127
給料支払小切手	141
給料を減らす	143
業界に名を馳せる	57
競合他社	58
(人に)協力する	81
許可をもらう	88
(〜を)拠出する	134
際立った	70
緊急の場合	47
勤労意欲を高める	78
くつろぐ	68
経営を続ける	143
契機	161
景気後退	171
(〜を)経験する	75
携帯電話	47
経費が若干掛かる	101
経費削減する	101
決意	62
欠陥	131
月給	117
見学をする	124
現在の(状況)	130
研修を担当する	46

検討する	113
(〜できて)光栄である	33, 71, 123
(〜の)後期に	107
貢献	54
(〜するのに)貢献する	70
広告	128
広告を放送する	128
考査	151
後退	77
好転する	77
後任者	37
心から感謝申し上げます	55
(〜を)ご自由に(おとりください)	88
(〜に)応える	140
ごちそうさま	65
この仕事に対してまだ何も知識がありませんが…	35
これから大変ご迷惑をおかけいたしますが…	35
これで終わり	158
今後のご活躍をお祈り申し上げます	55
今週末までに	132

さ行

サーバーへログインする	150
(〜時に)再開する	47
最高の出だしを切る	67
最後になりましたが	135
最後まで	81
最終的には	115
(〜に)最終報告する	120
最初の状態に戻す	131
(〜の)最新情報を伝える	130
最新の売上高	77
(〜で)最高値をつける	161
在宅勤務	151
裁判に持ち越す	81
(財務状況が)思わしくない	171
最安値をつける	161

索 引

(〜に)採用される	34
さて	72
さてでは	65
さらに詳しく	91
参加する	74
(〜に)参入する	68
(〜は)残念です	144
残念ながら〜である	143
賛否	103
仕上げを行なう	130
(〜での)シェアを伸ばす	115
シェアを広げる	107, 120
自家用	104
時間との勝負が求められる	54
時間をさいて〜する	134
(〜に)刺激を加える	127
仕事内容を書いたもの	116
仕事に精通する	41
(〜を)辞退する	103
実際に〜を見る	124
実地訓練	47
(〜に)質問する	41
質問を受け付ける	85
実用可能な	147
〜しておく	132
シミュレーションを行なう	138
使命	91
社内の	108
社内のお知らせ事項	150
社用車	104
(〜に)従事する	54
就職活動を始める	34
就職する	34
修正する	131
住宅手当	117
受注に対応する	141
需要に応える	154
準備中で	167
障害、問題を防ぐ	167
昇給	151
(〜という)条件をもってすれば	113
証言を求められる	81
詳細について検討する	164
(〜について)詳細を検討する	120
上昇	165
職を失わせる	112
処方箋	87
(〜を)知らされる	80
(〜を)知らせる	130
人員削減をする	143
真剣に〜を考える	154
人事管理	116
人事部	116
辛抱する	57
信頼のおける	68
救う	54
スケジュールの確認をする	158
捨てる	131
すべてがうまくいったとして	88
すべてが含まれる	90
すべて試みる	112
〜する以外方法がない	54
製造時間	140
製薬の	87
積極的に〜してください	47
説明書を回覧する	116
(〜を)説明する	150
宣誓証言	80
専門的な経験	53
(〜を)専門とする	96
戦略	153
早期退職プログラム	144
創業	84
そうすることに価値のある投資	65
(〜により)訴訟が起きる	80
(〜を)率先して行なう	153
それでは	65
それに加えて〜	117

尊敬の念を持って付き合う............................65

た行

(〜を)第一に考える............................93
耐久性............................137
(〜の)対象となる............................151
退職後に............................75
(〜を)大切にする............................75
大胆な............................70
(〜を)代表して............................43
代表する............................137
助け出す............................54
(〜に)頼る............................171
(〜を)担当する............................120
知恵を絞る............................148
(〜とは)違う............................91
着工する............................88
中規模の............................87
昼食休憩をとる............................47
直前の変更............................97
ちょっと時間をくれない?............................37
通勤する............................151
停滞する............................161
適応すること............................103
テスト結果を報告する............................137
(〜が)出揃う............................147
手間のかからない............................96
転換期............................75
(〜は)電話で対応可............................97
電話の内線番号............................38
どうか、ご一考ください............................100
倒産する............................144
同時に............................91
どうぞよろしくお願いいたします............................35
同僚............................71
ドタキャン............................97
特許侵害に関わる訴訟............................80
途方もない............................140
努力が実る............................75

な行

長く続くパートナーシップを培っていく............................125
何かございましたら............................98
(〜のもと)成り立っている............................93
慣れること............................103
なんとかやっていく............................71
何としても............................171
(〜社以上の、…の)ニーズに応える............................98
〜に関して言えば............................138
2シフト体制が組まれている............................51
忍耐............................62
任務に就く............................40
値上がりに向かう............................165
(〜を)願って............................141
ネットワークが障害を起こす............................54
年間売上高............................85

は行

(〜を)把握している............................130
(価格〜の)配当金を支払う............................161
(〜するよう)励む............................44
(〜から)始めさせていただきます............................160
(〜の)柱となる............................44
働きすぎだった............................108
発行済み普通株............................161
発表する............................144
話し合いが始まる............................164
話し合いを持つ............................147
話をしてもらう............................72
(〜に)話を持ちかける............................151
販売員............................60
ビジネスが回復し始めないと............................171
(〜年にわたり、…で(通常は「地域」が入る))
　ビジネスをしている............................98
引越し費用............................117
(〜に)引っ越す............................71
必要なメンテナンスを行なう............................51
必要に応じて〜対応可............................97
一株あたり............................161

索 引

人に～をしてもらう 158
一人ひとりの 144
日々の忠誠 58
評価する 120
評判 123
品質水準を満たす 44
増える経費 112
不調の 78
2日間休暇をとる 51
物流管理 108
太っ腹 113
プラス思考をする 78
不良品 140
プログラム（活動）をとりまとめる 153
プロジェクトがうまくいく 115
（プロジェクトに）参加する 134
閉鎖する 112
ベストを尽す 68
ペンディングです 88
（～を）報告できてうれしい 138
報道機関へ発表する 164
法務部 80
訪問を楽しみにする 123
ボーナスを出す 141
本日まで 60

ま行

（～に）優る 103
またどこかで会う 41
～まで 138
まとめる 113
（～の）味方である 77
短い休憩をとる 128
見通し 123
皆さん、ご苦労様 157
（～に）向かう 54
（～で）報われる 75

名刺 98
目指すもの 91
面会する時間をさく 119
元がとれる 101
問題を緩和させる 107

や行

役員 43, 58
休みをとる 158
薬局で購入できる 87
唯一の手段である 112
（～の）有利である 77
優良な 120
ゆっくり考える 104
ゆっくりと楽しむ 64
（～に）良い影響が働く 165
良い経験 125
良い結果 125
よい条件を追い求めて転職する 78
（～の）要求を満たす 91
ようやく、じかに会う 123
よく検討する 103
横ばい 165
予定を忘れないように
　カレンダーに書き込んでおく 111
喜んで～する 138

ら行

楽観視する 77
理念 153
連絡する 88
労働時間が長くなる 104

わ行

和解を申し出る 81
私は皆さんととても楽しく仕事を
　させてもらっています 68

ビジネスで使える
英語の1分間スピーチ

2006年11月6日　初版発行
2015年9月30日　4刷発行

著者
小坂貴志（こさか・たかし）
ジョン・ワンダリー（John Wunderley）
© Takashi Kosaka and John Wunderley, 2006

KENKYUSHA
〈検印省略〉

発行者
関戸雅男

発行所
株式会社　研究社
〒102-8152　東京都千代田区富士見2-11-3
電話　営業（03）3288-7777（代）　編集（03）3288-7711（代）
振替　00150-9-26710
http://www.kenkyusha.co.jp/

印刷所
研究社印刷株式会社

装丁・本文デザイン
亀井昌彦（株式会社 シータス）

CD ナレーター
Steve Martin
Helen Morrison

ISBN978-4-327-43058-0　C2082　Printed in Japan